ZEST

FRESH & VIBRANT RECIPES FOR CITRUS FRUIT

ZEST

FRESH & VIBRANT RECIPES FOR CITRUS FRUIT

RYLAND PETERS & SMALL

Senior Designer Megan Smith
Editor Kate Eddison
Editorial Director Julia Charles
Production Manager Gordana Simakovic
Creative Director Leslie Harrington
Indexer Vanessa Bird

First published in 2025 by
Ryland Peters & Small
20–21 Jockey's Fields, London
WC1R 4BW
and
1452 Davis Bugg Road
Warrenton, NC 27589

www.rylandpeters.com
email: euregulations@rylandpeters.com

10 9 8 7 6 5 4 3 2 1

Recipe collection compiled by Julia Charles.
Text © Valerie Aikman-Smith, Ghillie Basan,
Adriano di Petrillo, Ursula Ferrigno, Amy Ruth
Finegold, Liz Franklin, Felipe Fuentes Cruz,
Dunja Gulin, Victoria Hall, Carol Hilker, Kathy
Kordalis, Jenny Linford, Theo A. Michaels, Louise
Pickford, James Porter, Sarah Randall, Annie Rigg,
Shelagh Ryan, Laura Santini, María José Sevilla,
Will Torrent, Jenny Tschiesche, Laura Washburn
Hutton and Ryland Peters & Small 2025

Design and photography © Ryland Peters & Small
2025. All recipes in this book have been previously
published, see pages 174–176 for full credits.

Printed in China.

FSC
www.fsc.org
MIX
Paper | Supporting
responsible forestry
FSC® C106563

ISBN: 978-1-78879-686-6

A CIP record for this book is available from the
British Library. US Library of Congress cataloging-
in-Publication Data has been applied for.

The authorised representative in the EEA is
Authorised Rep Compliance Ltd., Ground Floor,
71 Lower Baggot Street, Dublin, D02 P593, Ireland
www.arccompliance.com

NOTES
• All spoon measurements are level unless
otherwise specified
5 ml = 1 teaspoon
15 ml = 1 tablespoon
• Uncooked or partially cooked eggs should
not be served to the very old, frail, young
children, pregnant women or those with
compromised immune systems.
• When a recipe calls for the grated zest
of citrus fruit, buy unwaxed fruit and wash
well before using.
• Ovens should be preheated to the specified
temperatures.
• To sterilize preserving jars, wash them in
hot, soapy water and rinse in boiling water.
Place in a large saucepan and cover with hot
water. With the saucepan lid on, bring the water
to the boil and continue boiling for 15 minutes.
Turn off the heat and leave the jars in the hot
water until just before they are to be filled. Invert
the jars onto a clean dish towel to dry. Sterilize
the lids for 5 minutes, by boiling (remove any
rubber seals first). Jars should be filled and
sealed while they are still hot.

CONTENTS

INTRODUCTION

Citrus fruits are quite possibly the most essential family of ingredients to cook with. They satisfy almost every part of the palate – sweet, sour, bitter, and are umami-enhancing. This fresh and vibrant collection of recipes explores the myriad uses of oranges, lemons, limes, grapefruit and more to provide a source of delight and inspiration in your kitchen all year round. From a quick squeeze of lemon juice over a plated dish to a rich and complex overnight marinade, citrus fruits have a magical ability to be both the star of the show or to quietly enhance and elevate both flavour and texture.

Oranges, grapefruit, lemons, limes and the lesser known pomelos and citron are all types of citrus fruit. They share a unique feature, a juicy pulp inside a leathery skin (known as peel or rind). Inside the peel, the flesh is divided into eight or more segments. Each of these contains miniscule liquid-filled pouches and seeds (though farmers have over the decades developed ways of growing seedless varieties). Any citrus fruit once cut to reveal a cross section is a thing of beauty, so delicate and intricate – no wonder slices are so often used to garnish savoury plates, cakes, desserts and drinks.

Citrus fruits grow abundantly on trees, bushes or even shrubs in the warm regions of the world. They were first found in southern China and other parts of Asia, and it was then Arab traders who brought citrus fruits to the Middle East, Africa and eventually they reached Europe via Spain – Seville bitter oranges are some of the most prized in the world. It was then European explorers who brought the fruits to the Americas in the 1500s and farmers there were able to cultivate them and establish luxuriant groves. Citrus can also thrive in the wild or even in private gardens, given the right conditions and care.

The sour, tangy quality of citrus fruit has the unique ability to lift every food it touches, adding acidity. Just a squeeze or a splash of juice can make salad dressings brighter, fish taste fresher, or add an instant and delightful tang to balance out anything too sweet or too salty. It can even make a pizza crust crispier and baked goods feel lighter in texture. The versatility of citrus fruit as an ingredient is unsurpassed – consider aromatic Asian-style curries, vibrant Mexican-inspired salsas, South American ceviche, tangy Indian pickles and North Africa tagines, none of these dishes would succeed without the addition of lemons, limes and oranges; whether it's just juice or the whole flesh and zest. Citrus skins themselves provide oil that can be used as a flavouring and rinds of zest can be candied with sugar to enjoy as sweet treat or as a baking ingredient.

In this book you will discover from a wide range of appetizing savoury and sweet recipes for every taste and occasion. Choose from fresh noodle salads and light seafood dishes to slow-cooked and meats as well as satisfying vegetable and pulse (legume) dishes. Discover simple home bakes as well as moreish desserts and refreshing drinks and cocktails. Why not bring some citrusy sunshine into your own home cooking every day?

1

SMALL PLATES
& APPETIZERS

ORANGE-MARINATED GREEN OLIVES

In Andalucía, where the olive has always taken centre stage at the table, marinating olives at the beginning of winter was a job home cooks felt proud to do and they tended to follow their own family's particular recipe. Today cured olives are easy to find in every local market, marinated in varying ways with many different aromatics; sometimes vinegar is added, but they are always tasty and very moreish. To make things easy for you here, a jar of manzanilla olives, so typical of the city of Sevilla, is used.

2 oranges
3 tablespoons Spanish extra virgin
    olive oil
1 teaspoon sherry vinegar
2 teaspoons white sesame seeds
1 teaspoon freshly ground
    black pepper
400 g/14 oz. manzanilla olives
    from a jar, drained and rinsed
a few small mint leaves

SERVES 8–10

Wash the oranges and grate and juice one of them. Set the other orange aside.

In a bowl, using a hand whisk, mix the orange juice and zest with the olive oil and the vinegar.

Peel the second orange, removing all the pith, and use a small knife to cut it into segments.

In a small frying pan/skillet, toast the sesame seeds until they take on a little colour and release their nutty aroma.

In a serving bowl, mix the toasted sesame seeds, black pepper, olives, orange segments and mint leaves before adding the liquid. Blend well.

These will keep in the fridge for several days.

PEPPERED PAN-FRIED OLIVES

Jewelled bright-green Italian Castelvetrano olives are perfect for pan frying. Mixed with citrus and salty capers, they offer a vibrant taste of the Italian countryside.

2 tablespoons olive oil
225 g/8 oz. Castelvetrano olives
2 slices of dried tangerine or orange
½ teaspoon freshly ground
    black pepper
2 teaspoons salted capers

SERVES 4–6

Heat the olive oil in a frying pan/skillet over a medium heat. Add the olives, dried tangerine slices, pepper and salted capers, and fry for 3–4 minutes.

Transfer to a serving bowl and serve immediately.

SALT-BAKED HERITAGE BEETROOT & MANGO LETTUCE CUPS
WITH LIME & NERIGOMA DRESSING

Salt-baking seems to intensify the sweetness of beetroot. If you can manage to find different coloured beetroots, it makes this a very beautiful dish. Served in lettuce cups, it makes a special dinner party starter.

800 g/4 cups coarse sea salt
3 egg whites
4 candy-striped and yellow
   beetroots/beets
3½ tablespoons olive oil
freshly squeezed juice of 2 limes
1 teaspoon caster/granulated sugar
1 small red onion, sliced
1 large ripe but firm tomato,
   roughly chopped
1 ripe mango, peeled, pitted
   and diced
a small of handful of freshly
   chopped coriander/cilantro
sea salt and freshly ground
   black pepper
iceberg or Little Gem lettuce cups
mint leaves, to garnish

DRESSING
4 tablespoons nerigoma
   (Japanese sesame paste)
grated zest and freshly squeezed
   juice of 1 lime
1 fat garlic clove, finely grated

SERVES 4

Preheat the oven to 190°C (375°F) Gas 5.

Put the salt into a large bowl and mix in the egg whites. Spread about one-third of the mixture in a thin layer on a lined sheet pan. Place the beetroots close together, and then pat the remaining salt mixture over the beetroots to cover them. Bake for 1 hour until they are soft when tested with the point of a knife.

Meanwhile, mix the olive oil, lime juice and sugar in a large bowl. Season.

When the beetroots are cooked, give the salt crust a good bash with a rolling pin, and remove them.

Once the beetroots are cool enough, gently peel them and cut them into dice.

Drop them into the lime dressing whilst they are still warm, and leave to cool completely.

Add the onion, tomato and mango to the dressing and stir in the freshly chopped coriander.

Whisk all the ingredients for the nerigoma dressing together with 3–4 tablespoons of water.

Peel away layers of the lettuce to make cups and fill with the beetroot mixture. Garnish with mint leaves, and serve with the dressing.

HOME-CURED DUCK 'PROSCIUTTO'
WITH ROCKET & ORANGE VINAIGRETTE

This is, of course, not really prosciutto… but it is home cured and makes a fabulous dish to share. It takes a good few days to cure and then needs another few days to rest, but it's a great way of preserving a duck breast to use over a couple of weeks. Here it is served with a side of rocket dressed with a simple orange vinaigrette and a few Parmesan shavings. Once it starts to dry out too much to enjoy on its own, it works nicely diced and fried to add to pasta or in a stew. Note that the curing time will need to increase, the larger the duck breast you are using.

1 x 250-g/9-oz. duck breast
2 tablespoons freshly squeezed orange juice, plus a little finely grated orange zest to garnish
4 tablespoons extra virgin olive oil
1 tablespoon cider vinegar
sea salt and freshly ground black pepper
a few handfuls of rocket/arugula, to serve

CURING SALT MIXTURE
400 g/2 cups coarse sea salt
50 g/½ cup demerara/turbinado sugar
1 tablespoon freshly ground black pepper
1 dried bay leaf, ground to a powder with a pestle and mortar

SERVES 12

Trim the duck breast of any trailing bits of fat, and if it has a very thick layer of fat on top, lightly trim this as well. Use a sharp knife to score the breast skin in diagonal lines, being careful not to pierce the flesh.

To make the curing salt mixture, simply mix together the salt, sugar, black pepper and ground bay leaf in a small bowl.

Choose a dish of material resistant to salt (ceramic or glass is best) into which the duck breast will fit snugly. Scatter one-third of the curing salt mixture in the bottom (or enough to create a complete layer), then lay the duck flesh-side down and cover with the remaining mixture. Add more salt if any of the duck is exposed, you need it to be fully encased. Cover the top of the dish with clingfilm/plastic wrap and refrigerate for 3 days.

After 3 days the duck will have shrunk a little and be much firmer. Rinse off the salt, pat it with paper towels until fully dry and then loosely wrap it in baking parchment (you don't want it to be airtight, it needs a little air to allow the moisture to escape). Return it to the fridge for a further 5 days.

When ready to serve, make the dressing by whisking together the orange juice, olive oil and vinegar until emulsified and season with a pinch each of salt and pepper.

Slice the duck very thinly, starting at the thinner end and cutting at an angle. Arrange the slices on a plate with the rocket, and dress with the orange vinaigrette and a sprinkle of grated orange zest.

You can store any leftover duck, unsliced, in the fridge in an airtight container so that it doesn't dry out.

HOME-CURED ANCHOVIES

Throughout the Mediterranean it is the cheap, small fish that form a major part of the staple diet. Abundant in local waters and full of healthy fats, anchovies are delicious once cured and served with some really good bread and a glass of wine. If you can't find fresh anchovies, sprats work just as well and belong to the same family of fish. Here, smoked sea salt is used to cure these, which gives a pleasing hint of smokiness, but regular coarse sea salt will work just as well.

12 fresh anchovies or sprats
about 50 g/¼ cup coarse smoked
   sea salt or coarse sea salt
100 ml/7 tablespoons sherry
   vinegar
freshly squeezed juice of 1 lemon
a 5-cm/2-inch piece of lemon zest
1 garlic clove, thickly sliced
2 dried bay leaves
a pinch of Greek dried oregano
250 ml/1 cup light olive oil
a few pink peppercorns, crushed,
   to garnish (optional)
lemon wedges, for squeezing
chunks of rustic bread, to serve

*a 750-ml/3-cup capacity sealable
   glass jar, sterilized*

SERVES 8

Fillet the anchovies or sprats, discarding the head, bones and guts (or ask your fishmonger to do this for you when you buy them).

Scatter one-quarter of the salt on a plate that won't react with the salt (ceramic or glass is best). Layer the fillets on top, salting between each layer. These don't need to be fully encased in salt, so you should have enough, but use a little more if you feel you need to. Cover and refrigerate for 6 hours.

Put the sherry vinegar and lemon juice in a small bowl and whisk to combine.

Remove the sprats from the fridge, rinse the salt off them and pat them dry with paper towels. Put them in a shallow dish and pour over the sherry vinegar and lemon juice mixture. Shuffle them around to ensure they are all submerged, cover and let them pickle in the fridge for 1 hour.

After an hour, remove them from the pickling liquor, shaking off some of the excess.

Add the lemon zest, garlic, bay leaves and oregano to the sterilized jar. Add the cured fillets and pour in the olive oil to cover. These are best eaten after a day or two, so that they have time to soak in the flavours, but refrigerate them until ready to serve and eat them within 3 days.

To serve, lay the anchovies out flat on a plate, leave for 10 minutes to take the fridge chill off and drizzle with some of the oil from the jar (if the oil has solidified just leave 1–2 tablespoon of it to liquefy at room temperature) and scatter over some crushed pink peppercorns (if using). Add a few lemon wedges for squeezing and serve with chunks of rustic bread and a glass of white wine.

STUFFED VINE LEAVES
WITH ZINGY GARLIC-HERB DRESSING

These dolmades are made throughout the Balkans and Middle East. There are many variations, including this one with a very simple zest-flavoured filling and zingy garlic and herb dressing. The filling here is a mixture of rice and quinoa and a lot of herbs and citrus juices as they make for a lighter dish, and one suitable for vegans, vegetarians and flexitarians alike.

4 tablespoons olive oil, plus extra to drizzle

1 bunch spring onions/scallions, finely chopped

1 onion, finely chopped

2 garlic cloves, crushed

250 g/generous 1¼ cups short-grain rice

200 ml/scant 1 cup vegetable stock

100 g/½ cup cooked mixed tricolore quinoa grains

½ bunch coriander/cilantro, finely chopped

½ bunch dill, finely chopped

½ bunch mint, leaves picked and chopped

finely grated zest and freshly squeezed juice of 1 lime

1 lemon, sliced, plus freshly squeezed juice of 1 lemon

250 g/9 oz. vine leaves, from a jar

sea salt and freshly ground black pepper

DRESSING

3 garlic cloves, crushed

1 teaspoon Dijon/French mustard

finely grated zest and freshly squeezed juice of 1 lemon

a pinch of sugar

60 ml/¼ cup olive oil

a handful each of flat-leaf parsley, dill and mint, finely chopped

SERVES 4

Heat the olive oil in a sauté pan, add the spring onions, onion and garlic and sauté for 10–15 minutes, until softened and caramelized.

Add the rice, cook for 2 minutes, then add the stock and stir. Lower the heat and simmer for about 5 minutes until the rice soaks up the liquid.

Remove the pan from the heat, stir in the cooked quinoa and set aside to rest for at least 10 minutes.

Add the coriander, dill, mint, lime zest and lime juice, mix to combine and season with salt and pepper.

Spread 4–5 vine leaves across the base of a 22-cm/9-inch flameproof casserole dish. Add the lemon slices and squeeze over the lemon juice.

Lay a vine leaf flat on a plate with veins facing up and shiny side down. Add 1 tablespoon of filling in the centre, fold the sides of the vine leaf inwards, then roll up the vine leaf to enclose the filling.

Transfer to the dish, placing the stuffed vine leaves in a row, one next to the other.

Repeat the process, add to the layers until all the filling is used.

Drizzle over some olive oil and cover the stuffed vine leaves with a plate (so that they don't fall apart while cooking). Add enough warm or hot water to completely cover them. Simmer over a low heat for 40–50 minutes until the rice is done and the vine leaves are tender.

For the dressing, add the garlic, mustard, lemon zest, lemon juice and sugar to a food processor. With the machine on the lowest setting, drizzle in all the olive oil until it's emulsified, then stir in the herbs.

When the vine leaves are ready, remove from heat and set them aside to cool in the pot.

Serve drizzled with the zingy garlic-herb dressing.

TOASTED MIXED GRAINS
WITH LEMON LABNE

Absolute heaven on a plate! It's hard to know where to begin – the grains (which are pre-toasted for added flavour), the lemony and creamy home-made labne, all finished with sweet-and-sour pomegranate molasses.

50 g/⅓ cup spelt grain
50 g/⅓ cup faro
60 g/⅓ cup quinoa
60 g/⅓ cup bulgur
1 x 400-g/14-oz. can green
  lentils, drained
80 g/⅔ cup pistachios,
  coarsely chopped
75 g/½ cup dried apricots,
  coarsely chopped
1 red onion, thinly sliced
150 g/5½ oz. mixed micro herbs
  and leaves

LEMON LABNE
500 g/2¼ cups Greek yogurt
grated zest and freshly squeezed
  juice of 1 lemon
1 garlic clove, crushed
1½ teaspoons salt
freshly ground black pepper

POMEGRANATE DRESSING
80 ml/⅓ cup extra virgin olive oil
2 tablespoons red wine vinegar
freshly squeezed juice of 1 lemon
2 tablespoons pomegranate
  molassess
½ pomegranate, seeds only
a pinch of za'atar
sea salt and freshly ground
  black pepper

TO SERVE
1 tablespoon za'atar
½ pomegranate, seeds only
olive oil, to drizzle

SERVES 4–6

Start the lemon labne the night before. Combine the yogurt, lemon zest and juice, garlic, salt and freshly ground black pepper (to taste) in a bowl, then transfer to a sieve/strainer lined with muslin/cheesecloth, place over a bowl to catch the liquid and refrigerate overnight to drain.

Dry-roast the spelt and faro in a frying pan/skillet for 1–2 minutes until nutty and fragrant.

Tip the toasted spelt and faro into a saucepan, cover with boiling water and simmer for 15–20 minutes until tender, then drain and refresh under cold running water. Drain well and transfer to a large bowl.

Meanwhile, cook the quinoa in a pan of boiling salted water for 4–5 minutes, then add the bulgur and cook for another minute. Drain well and refresh under cold running water. Add to spelt mixture.

Make the pomegranate dressing directly in the serving bowl by whisking all the ingredients together, then season to taste.

In the same dish add the green lentils, pistachios, dried apricots, red onion and all the cooked grains. Season to taste and toss to combine. Gently mix through all the micro herbs and greens.

To serve, on small plates place a dollop of labne to the side and sprinkle with za'atar. Add some of the grainy mix, top with pomegranate seeds, then drizzle with olive oil.

SEA BASS CRUDO

The fish, clams and shellfish served in southern Italy are very fresh and simply prepared – crudo, meaning 'raw', accurately defines how they like things. This is a great dish for gatherings, a sharing starter, or on its own with an Aperol Spritz.

4 very fresh sea bass fillets
freshly squeezed juice of 1 lemon
freshly squeezed juice of 1 lime
150 g/5½ oz. red radishes
150 g/5½ oz. mooli/daikon radish
1 small red onion
handful of flat-leaf parsley
1 tablespoon red peppercorns, crushed
sea salt
olive oil, to drizzle

SERVES 4

Thinly slice the sea bass and place neatly on a serving plate. Drizzle with half the lemon and lime juices and add a sprinkle of salt.

Very thinly slice the radishes and red onion. Roughly chop the parsley. Combine these together, then mix with the remaining citrus juices and a drizzle of olive oil.

Scatter the mixture over the fish, then drizzle over a little more olive oil. Add the crushed red peppercorns, and serve.

POISSON CRU

This is Tahiti's answer to poke or ceviche, made using freshly squeezed coconut milk and lime juice. It is typically made using tuna that has been well rinsed in salt water.

900 g/2 lb. very fresh firm fish fillets
1 tablespoon sea salt
1 green (bell) pepper
1 large cucumber, deseeded and roughly peeled (some skin left on)
2 x 400-g/14-oz. cans coconut milk
1 large carrot half cut into matchsticks
freshly squeezed juice of 7 limes (approx 120 ml/½ cup lime juice)
5 tomatoes
1 spring onion/scallion, thinly sliced, to garnish (optional)

SERVES 4

Cut the fish into 2 x 5-cm/¾ x 2-inch pieces. Rinse under running water or soak it in salted water for about 5 minutes, then drain and place in a large glass or stainless steel mixing bowl.

Cut the pepper, cucumber, tomatoes and half the carrot into 2 x 5-cm/¾ x 2-inch pieces

Sprinkle the rock salt over the fish pieces and mix. Add the (bell) pepper, cucumber and coconut milk. Gently mix together with your hands to avoid breaking up the fish. Add the carrot pieces and lime juice; gently mix again. Add the tomatoes and gently mix again.

Wipe the rim of the bowl down and cover with clingfilm/plastic wrap. Marinate in the fridge for a minimum of 2 hours to allow the flavours to infuse.

Before serving, cut the remaining carrot half into matchsticks and thinly slice the spring onion/scallion. Scatter on top as a garnish.

CITRUS-MARINATED CEVICHE

This classic Mexican appetizer truly embraces the wonders of citrus flavours. The acidic juices essentially 'cook' the fish and at the same time impart their unique and tasty flavour. This dish can be made 2 days in advance, as long as very fresh fish is used.

450 g/1 lb. mixed raw white fish fillets, such as hake, haddock and sole, skinned and pin-boned (you can do this yourself with a pair of fish bone tweezers or ask your fishmonger)
freshly squeezed juice of 3 lemons
freshly squeezed juice of 3 limes
2 teaspoons freshly chopped oregano leaves
½ teaspoon cumin seeds
1 large ripe tomato, finely diced
1 small red onion, finely chopped
1 green chilli/chile, deseeded (optional) and finely chopped
a handful of fresh coriander/cilantro leaves, chopped
a handful of fresh mint leaves, chopped
sea salt and freshly ground black pepper
2 tablespoons olive oil

SERVES 4

Cut all the fish into 1-cm/½-inch cubes and place in a glass container or bowl with the lemon and lime juices and chopped oregano. Mix well, cover with clingfilm/plastic wrap and leave in the fridge for up to 12 hours (any longer and the fish will become very mushy).

Meanwhile, toast the cumin seeds for a couple of minutes in a dry frying pan/skillet set over a medium heat, shaking the pan and stirring constantly until fragrant. Remove the seeds from the pan and let cool.

Drain and discard the citrus juices from the fish. Put the fish into a clean bowl and mix with the toasted cumin seeds, chopped tomato, onion, chilli coriander and mint. Add salt and pepper to taste, drizzle over the oil and divide up into small bowls to serve.

Alternatively, at this stage, the fish mixture will keep for up to 2 days in the refrigerator in an airtight container.

SALMON ESCABECHE
WITH CELERY & CITRUS

A true marriage made in heaven. Escabeche is a Spanish method of searing fish or meat and then marinating it in a tangy citrus dressing. Do try this technique with other fresh fish – mackerel is divine.

2 tablespoons olive oil
4 boneless salmon fillets, skinned
2 shallots, sliced into thin rounds
2 fennel bulbs, trimmed and thinly
  sliced, reserve the fronds to
  garnish
4 celery stalks/sticks, as white
  as possible, thinly sliced
3 fresh bay leaves
4 garlic cloves, thinly sliced
grated zest of 2 lemons and freshly
  squeezed juice of 1
grated zest of 2 limes and freshly
  squeezed juice of 1
a handful of mint leaves
sea salt and freshly ground
  black pepper
crusty bread, to serve

SERVES 4

Heat the oil in a large non-stick frying pan/skillet. Season the salmon fillets with salt and fry over a medium heat for 3 minutes on each side until a little opaque. Set aside to rest.

Return the pan to the heat. Add the shallots, fennel, celery and bay leaves. Season with salt and pepper and cook for 5 minutes.

Add the garlic and cook for a further 2 minutes. Remove from the heat and add the citrus juice and zest and 4 tablespoons of water.

Add the fish to this citrus mixture and spoon the juices over the fish. Arrange on a platter with the mint leaves and fennel fronds.

Serve with crusty bread to mop up the juices.

TUNA CARPACCIO
WITH LEMON PARSLEY SAUCE

This delicious treatment of tuna can also be used with sea bass and swordfish. Your fishmonger will be able to slice the fresh fish very thinly for you – an opportunity to show off! This dish is enjoyed in the Sicilian town of Marsala, where the fish is sweet.

400 g/14 oz. fresh tuna, cut into very thin slices

4 tablespoons extra virgin olive oil (not too fruity)

freshly squeezed juice of 2 lemons, plus 1 lemon, sliced, to garnish

1 tablespoon freshly chopped oregano

2 tablespoons freshly chopped flat-leaf parsley

250 g/9 oz. rocket/arugula, spinach or chicory/endive (or a mixture of all three)

sea salt and freshly ground black pepper

SERVES 4

Place the tuna on a plate. Whisk together the oil, lemon juice, oregano, parsley, salt and pepper until emulsified.

Pour the sauce over the tuna. Cover and refrigerate for 1–2 hours, turning once during that period.

Arrange the leaves on a platter, top with tuna and serve garnished with lemon slices.

DEEP-FRIED BABY ARTICHOKES
WITH LEMON, MINT & ANCHOVY DRESSING

This is the perfect recipe for young artichokes when they are in season, which have no fiddly 'choke' to remove. The anchovies in this herby lemony dressing add a delicious piquancy to the dish.

12 small young artichokes
2 tablespoons lemon juice,
   for acidulating the water
2 lemons
groundnut/peanut oil,
   for deep-frying

BATTER
375 g/2¾ cups plus 1½ tablespoons
   '00' Italian flour or plain/
   all-purpose flour
a pinch of sea salt
125 ml/½ cup olive oil
80 ml/generous ⅓ cup sparkling
   water
1 UK large/US extra-large egg white

DRESSING
6 anchovy fillets in olive oil
a generous handful of mint leaves
1 tablespoon freshly squeezed
   lemon juice, or to taste
1 tablespoon red wine vinegar
120 ml/½ cup fruity extra virgin
   olive oil, or to taste

SERVES 4–6

Start by making the batter – there will be more than you need but it keeps well in the fridge. Sift the flour into a large bowl, add a pinch of salt and make a well in the centre. Pour in the olive oil, whisking until combined. Add the sparkling water and whisk again until combined. In a separate bowl, whisk the egg white to firm peaks and then gently fold this in. Cover and set the batter aside in the fridge until needed.

To make the anchovy dressing, drain and rinse the anchovies and pat dry. Add these to a food processor along with the rest of the dressing ingredients and blend to make a lovely green paste. Taste and add more oil or lemon juice, if needed.

To prepare the artichokes, use a sharp knife to trim and peel he stems and cut off the tops of the tough outer leaves at the point where their colour becomes dark. Cut the artichokes in half lengthways and remove the hairy choke if needed (in young artichokes there will not be any choke). Immerse the vegetables in a bowl of water acidulated with a little lemon juice.

Slice the whole lemons into fairly thin, even rounds – they will be deep-fried so don't make them so thin they will fall apart.

When ready to cook, drain the artichokes from their lemon water and pat dry with paper towels. Heat the groundnut oil in a deep-fryer or large pan to around 180°C (350°F).

Dip each artichoke in the batter and turn to give an even coating, then lift out to let the excess batter drain away. Lower carefully into the hot oil and deep-fry the artichokes in batches of 4–5 at a time until golden. Remove with a slotted spoon and drain on paper towels.

Batter and deep-fry the lemon slices in the same way.

Serve the hot artichokes and lemon slices with the anchovy dressing on a warmed plate and enjoy.

2

SOUPS & SALADS

VIETNAMESE NOODLE SOUP

Pho, pronounced 'fuh', is a staple all over Vietnam. It is thought to be an adaptation of the classic French beef casserole pot-au-feu, dating from the time when the country was part of French Indochina. There are many variations, but all use a citrus hit of lime.

1 onion, halved

4 cm/1½-inch piece of fresh ginger, cut in half, peel on

1 kg/2¼ lb. beef short ribs

1 bone marrow (approx. 200 g/7 oz.)

1 cinnamon stick

2 star anise

½ teaspoon fennel seeds

1 teaspoon coriander seeds

5 cloves

5 cardamom pods, crushed

2 tablespoons Thai fish sauce, or to taste

2 teaspoons palm sugar, or to taste

2 teaspoons salt, or to taste

150 g/2 cups rice noodles

1 tablespoon groundnut/peanut oil

150 g/5 oz. skirt steak

3 spring onions/scallions, thinly sliced diagonally

a handful each of fresh Thai basil leaves, mint leaves and coriander/cilantro leaves

freshly squeezed juice of 2 limes, plus lime wedges, to serve

1 Thai chilli/chile, thinly sliced

a baking sheet, lined

SERVES 4

Preheat the oven to 200°C (400°F) Gas 6.

Place the onion and ginger on the lined baking sheet and bake for 30 minutes until coloured.

Place the short ribs and marrow in a large, heavy saucepan and cover with cold water. Bring to the boil and remove any scum. Reduce the heat and simmer for 20 minutes. Drain the beef and bone marrow and rinse with cold water. Clean the pan.

Toast the spices in a dry frying pan/skillet until scented, then pound with a pestle and mortar.

Place the ribs and marrow along with the onion, ginger, spices, fish sauce, palm sugar and salt in the large pan. Pour enough cold water over to cover. Bring to the boil. Reduce the heat and simmer, uncovered, for 4 hours.

Strain the broth into a clean pan. Retain the meat from the ribs and marrow and discard the bones and aromatics. Top up the broth with cold water so you have 1 litre/4 cups in total.

Soak the rice noodles in cold water for 10 minutes.

Heat the oil in a frying pan/skillet and fry the steak for 4 minutes on each side. Slice while still warm.

Warm the broth and, if necessary, add more fish sauce, palm sugar and salt to taste.

Drain the noodles and add to the broth, then add the meat from the ribs and marrow, the sliced steak and all the remaining ingredients to the broth.

Serve with lime wedges on the side.

PORK DUMPLINGS IN LIME LEAF BROTH

This light and fragrant dish is surprisingly quick and simple to make. It's an excellent recipe for entertaining – you can make the dumplings ahead of time and cover with a damp cloth in the refrigerator.

1 tablespoon groundnut/peanut oil
300 g/10½ oz. minced/ground pork
5 tablespoons hoisin sauce
1 garlic clove, crushed
3 tablespoons fresh coriander/
    cilantro leaves, chopped
20 dumpling or wonton wrappers

BROTH
1 litre/4 cups chicken stock
3 slices of fresh ginger, peeled
    and cut into matchsticks
5 fresh makrut lime leaves, lightly
    crushed, plus extra, shredded,
    to garnish
2 tablespoons tamari soy sauce

SERVES 4

Heat the oil in a frying pan/skillet, add the minced pork and fry for 8 minutes, stirring, until browned.

To make the pork dumplings, combine the pork, hoisin sauce, garlic and coriander.

Place a tablespoon of the mixture in the centre of each wonton wrapper. Brush a little water around the edges of the wrappers and press the edges together to seal.

To make the lime leaf broth, place the chicken stock, ginger, lime leaves and soy sauce in a saucepan and simmer over medium–high heat for 3 minutes. Add the dumplings a few at a time and cook for 8 minutes, or until cooked through.

Place the dumplings in bowls and pour some of the broth over to serve. Garnish with shredded lime leaves and serve.

MEXICAN CHICKEN & LIME SOUP
WITH AVOCADO

This simple soup is a classic Mexican dish, with lime juice providing a lovely zingy freshness. Avocado is added at the end and this soup is typically served with a bowl of tortilla chips. If you can, always make your own chicken stock – it not only gives you a rich depth of nutritious flavour, but it also provides you with the shredded chicken meat for this particular recipe.

3 tablespoons olive oil
1 onion, finely chopped
2 garlic cloves, finely chopped
1 green chilli/chile, seeded and
    chopped
grated zest of 1 lime
½ teaspoon ground coriander
¼ teaspoon ground cumin
1½ litres/6 cups chicken stock
2 tomatoes, finely chopped
500 g/1 lb. 2 oz. shredded cooked
    chicken (this can be the meat
    from the chicken cooked to make
    the stock, if you make your own)
freshly squeezed juice of 2 limes
1 avocado, chopped
a large handful of cilantro/
    coriander leaves, chopped
sea salt and freshly ground
    black pepper
tortilla chips, to serve

SERVES 4

Heat the oil in a 4-litre/quart Dutch oven over a medium heat. Fry the onion, garlic, chilli, lime zest, spices, and some salt and pepper for 5–6 minutes until the onion is softened.

Add the stock and tomatoes and bring to the boil, then reduce the heat and simmer gently for 10 minutes until the tomatoes are softened.

Stir in the chicken and lime juice and simmer for a further 5 minutes until the chicken is heated through.

Divide amongst soup bowls, top each one with the chopped avocado and coriander leaves, and serve with a bowl of tortilla chips on the side.

PEA & HAM SOUP
WITH LEMON & THYME OIL

Pea and ham soup (also known as pease pudding) is made with dried split peas rather than fresh ones. A British favourite, this soup can be traced back to the Middle Ages when it was favoured by sailors who added salt pork to the broth for extra protein and flavour. It is still popular today, and the added swirl of zingy lemon and herb oil before serving gives it a lovely freshness.

400 g/2 cups split green peas
1 onion, finely chopped
1 carrot, finely chopped
2 celery stalks/sticks, finely
    chopped
2 garlic cloves, bashed
2 bay leaves, bashed
2 sprigs of rosemary, bashed
350-g/12-oz. piece of smoked
    bacon or pancetta, rind left on
sea salt and freshly ground
    black pepper
crusty bread, to serve

LEMON & THYME OIL
1 garlic clove
2 large sprigs of thyme,
    plus extra to serve
grated zest of 1 lemon,
    plus extra to serve
100 ml/7 tablespoons extra virgin
    olive oil

SERVES 6

Rinse the split peas thoroughly under cold water and shake dry. Place in a 4-litre/quart Dutch oven with 2 litres/quarts of cold water and bring to the boil. Simmer fast for 1 minute, removing any scum from the surface, then add all the remaining soup ingredients and bring to the boil. Reduce the heat, cover, and simmer for 1½–2 hours, or until the peas are really tender.

Season to taste (you may not need to add salt, as the bacon is already quite salty). Remove the bacon from the stock and cut away and discard the rind. Shred the meat, set aside, and keep warm.

Meanwhile, make the lemon and thyme oil. Place the garlic, thyme sprigs and lemon zest in a mortar and pestle with a little salt and pound together to release the flavours and oils. Transfer to a small saucepan, pour over the olive oil, and heat very gently for 10 minutes without allowing it to come to a boil. Set aside to cool, then strain the oil, discarding the aromatics.

Divide the soup amongst warm bowls and top with the shredded bacon. Drizzle over the oil and serve with a little extra thyme, lemon zest and freshly ground black pepper, with crusty bread on the side.

AVGOLEMONO
CHICKEN, LEMON & EGG SOUP

Every country has one recipe that is woven into the very fabric of its civilization and avgolemono is perhaps a dish that has been served at the kitchen table of every Greek person ever born. This warming soul food chicken soup is laced with fresh lemon juice and egg, which creates a creamy yet sharp flavour that is utterly unique. Legend says it can heal everything from a broken heart to a broken leg – you could try it for the first ailment, but perhaps opt for more modern medical practices for the second...

a 1.5-kg/3¼-lb. chicken
1.5–2 litres/6–8 cups water
   or chicken stock
2 dried bay leaves
4 sprigs of flat-leaf parsley
1 celery stalk/stick
200 g/1 cup Arborio risotto rice,
   rinsed
200 g/7 oz. halloumi, cut into
   2-cm/¾-inch dice and brought
   to room temperature
3 eggs
freshly squeezed juice of 1 lemon,
   plus extra to taste
sea salt and freshly ground
   black pepper
extra virgin olive oil, to drizzle
sprigs of dill, to garnish
rustic bread, to serve

SERVES 6

Put the chicken in a stockpot or large saucepan that is a snug fit but with some space. Add sufficient water (or stock, if using) to cover the chicken by about 5 cm/2 inches and set over a medium heat. Add the bay leaves, parsley sprigs and celery, bring to the boil, then reduce the heat and cook at a very gentle simmer for about 1½ hours.

After that time, turn off the heat, remove the chicken from the pot and set it aside on a carving plate or board and cover. Pass the stock through a sieve/strainer set over a large bowl and discard the bay leaves, parsley and celery.

Return the strained stock to the pan and set over a medium heat. Add the rice and cook for 15–20 minutes, or until the rice is just tender, then turn off the heat.

Shred one-quarter of the cooked chicken and add this to the pot along with 125 ml/½ cup cold water and the diced halloumi. (Save the remaining chicken to enjoy as leftovers.)

In a large mixing bowl, beat the eggs with the lemon juice, then push a ladle into the soup (avoiding any rice, chicken or halloumi) and, very slowly, pour the ladleful of soup into the beaten eggs, continuously whisking with a balloon whisk as you do. Repeat with a second ladleful. The aim is to temper the egg mixture to bring the temperature up without cooking it. If you pour the liquid in too quickly, you'll cook the eggs and it will curdle.

Once the eggs are tempered slowly pour the mixture back into the stockpot, stirring as you do. Taste the soup, and add more lemon juice and a little salt to taste.

If the soup needs warming, put it back over a low heat for a few minutes, stirring continuously, but don't let it simmer or it will curdle.

Once warmed through, ladle the soup into bowls, ensuring everyone gets chicken, rice and halloumi, then top each one up with more soup. Finish each bowl with a few grinds of black pepper, a pinch of salt and a drizzle of extra virgin olive oil, then garnish will dill sprigs and serve with rustic bread.

WHEATBERRIES, CHORIZO, ORANGE, OLIVE & RADICCHIO SALAD

If you can get blood oranges, they look just stunning in this recipe, but if they are not in season you can use normal oranges. This is one of those dishes that looks beautiful when you bring it to the table and tastes just as good.

4 blood oranges
1 red onion, thinly sliced
2 tablespoons olive oil, plus extra
    for frying
2 tablespoons runny honey
a pinch of dried chilli flakes/hot red
    pepper flakes
1 tablespoon cumin seeds, toasted
1 tablespoon coriander seeds,
    toasted
100 g/1 cup pitted Kalamata olives
200 g/generous 1 cup wheatberries
1 chorizo ring, chopped into discs
2 heads radicchio, leaves separated
20 g/¾ oz. flat-leaf parsley,
    leaves picked

SERVES 4

Peel and chop the oranges, and place in a serving dish. Add the sliced red onion, olive oil, honey, dried chilli flakes, toasted cumin and coriander seeds and black olives. Stir together and set aside to marinate for at least an hour in the serving dish.

While that all those flavours are melding, cook the wheatberries according to the package instructions, then drain and add to the orange mixture while still warm – this will help all the flavours infuse more.

Heat a drizzle of oil in a large frying pan/skillet. Cook the chorizo slices for 4–5 minutes until they are sizzling. Add to the serving dish with all the other ingredients, reserving the pan juices.

Finish with the radicchio leaves and flat-leaf parsley, and serve drizzled with all the chorizo pan juices.

SUN-BLUSH TOMATO, ORANGE & BURRATA SALAD

Gloriously simple to put together, this bright and colourful dish offers a Mediterranean-inspired combination of colours, textures and flavours.

2 large oranges
24 sun-blush/semi-dried cherry
    tomato halves
2 burrata cheeses or good-quality
    fresh mozzarella cheeses
a handful of basil leaves
freshly ground black pepper
extra virgin olive oil, to drizzle

SERVES 4

Peel the oranges, making sure to trim off all the white pith, and cut into even, thick slices.

Place the orange slices on a large serving dish, then scatter over the sun-blush tomato halves.

Tear the burrata into chunks and layer on top of the orange slices.

Drizzle with extra virgin olive oil and season with pepper. Top with basil leaves and serve at once.

FREEKAH & HERB SALAD
WITH PRESERVED LEMON & BLACK OLIVES

Roasted shallots with a touch of cinnamon serve as a bed for the freekah, crisp cucumber, tomatoes, olives and the intense-citrus-yet-mellow preserved lemon. For an extra element, crumble over some feta or add pan-fried halloumi.

8 shallots, halved
2 tablespoons olive oil
a pinch of ground cinnamon
a pinch of dried oregano
200 g/7 oz. freekah, rinsed
50 g/generous ⅓ cup almonds,
    coarsely chopped and toasted
1 large cucumber, cubed
200 g/2 cups cherry tomatoes,
    quartered
1 small bunch each dill, coriander/
    cilantro, mint and parsley,
    leaves picked
sea salt and freshly ground
    black pepper
feta or pan-fried halloumi, to serve
    (optional)

DRESSING
100 g/1 cup pitted black olives,
    halved
1 preserved lemon, pith and
    flesh discarded, skin rinsed
    and finely chopped
1 garlic clove, crushed
60 ml/¼ cup olive oil
a pinch of ground cinnamon
    (optional)
freshly squeezed juice of
    1–2 lemons, to taste
1 teaspoon honey, or to taste

SERVES 4

Preheat the oven to 180°C (350°F) Gas 4.

Spread the shallots on a small baking sheet. Drizzle with the olive oil, sprinkle with cinnamon and oregano and season to taste. Roast in the preheated oven for 40–45 minutes until the shallots are tender and caramelized.

Meanwhile, bring 400 ml/1¾ cups water and 1 teaspoon salt to the boil in a saucepan over a medium–high heat. Add the freekah, stir, bring back to the boil and cover with a lid. Reduce the heat to low and cook for 25–30 minutes until the freekah is tender and the water evaporates. Drain and transfer to a bowl.

Mix the dressing ingredients in a serving dish, then add the shallots, freekah, cucumber and tomatoes and mix well. Check for seasoning, then add the herbs and scatter over the almonds.

Serve with the addition of crumbled feta or pan-fried halloumi, if liked.

ORANGE, HONEY & OLIVE OIL SALAD

Often you will see toasted bread with fresh tomatoes, sprinkled with olive oil and a little sea salt served for breakfast in bars and hotels in Andalucía. However, fresh oranges also work beautifully drizzled with olive oil and honey – the sweetness of the honey and citrus fruit complements the extra virgin olive oil.

4 oranges
3 teaspoons runny honey
freshly squeezed juice of ½ orange
3 tablespoons Spanish extra virgin
    olive oil
a few mint leaves, to garnish

SERVES 4

Cut away all the skin and pith from the oranges and, using a serrated knife, cut each orange into 5–6 thin slices. Arrange the fruit on a large serving plate.

Blend the honey with the orange juice in a small bowl, then drizzle over the fruit, followed by the olive oil. Garnish with a few mint leaves and serve.

THAI TOMATO SALAD

This Thai-style salad, with its salty-sweet, chilli-flavoured dressing, is easy to put together. Serve it as a pleasingly textured side dish with a rich beef and coconut-milk curry and steamed rice.

16 cherry tomatoes, quartered
200 g/2 cups sugar snap peas,
    trimmed and halved
1 courgette/zucchini, grated
1 carrot, peeled and grated
2 tablespoons Thai fish sauce
1 tablespoon rice vinegar
2 teaspoons sweet chilli sauce
freshly squeezed juice of ½ lime
50 g/⅓ cup roasted peanuts,
    finely ground
a handful of Thai basil leaves,
    to garnish

SERVES 4

Toss together the cherry tomatoes, sugar snap peas, courgette and carrot in a serving dish.

To make the dressing, mix together the Thai fish sauce, vinegar, sweet chilli sauce and lime juice. Pour over the salad.

Mix in the ground peanuts, garnish with Thai basil leaves and serve.

TAMARIND RICE SALAD
WITH CRAB & GREEN CHILLIES

Tamarind, with its sour-sweet tang akin to apricots and lemons, really brings this rice and green chilli salad to life. The dish is full of different textures and the carmargue rice, cooling cucumber, puffed spelt, luxurious crab meat and spicy green chillies make this salad perfect for entertaining, be it a summer barbecue, a light lunch or part of a dinner party with friends.

200 g/generous 1 cup red carmargue rice, cooked according to package instructions and cooled
1 long cucumber, halved, seeds removed and cut in half moons
½ red onion, thinly sliced
20 g/scant 1 cup puffed spelt
40 g/scant ⅓ cup peanuts, coarsely crushed
400 g/14 oz. white crab meat
a handful each of mint and coriander/cilantro, leaves picked
1 long green chilli/chile, thinly sliced diagonally
4 spring onions/scallions, thinly sliced
lime wedges, to serve

DRESSING
1 tablespoon tamarind paste
20 g/1 cup mint
20 g/1 cup coriander/cilantro
1 long green chilli/chile, finely chopped
1 garlic clove, crushed
1 teaspoon ground cumin
freshly squeezed juice of 2 limes
1 teaspoon honey, or to taste
3 tablespoons olive oil
2 tablespoons good-quality mayonnaise

SERVES 4

In a serving bowl place the rice, cucumber and red onion. Set aside.

Make the dressing by mixing all the ingredients together, taste for seasoning and add 3 tablespoons water to loosen. Add to the rice mixture and set aside to infuse.

Meanwhile, preheat the oven to 180°C (350°F) Gas 4.

Place the puffed spelt and peanuts on a baking sheet and toast in the preheated oven until golden. Allow to cool.

Add the crab to the rice mixture, then top with the toasted puffed spelt and peanuts. Add the herbs, green chilli and spring onions. Serve with lime wedges for squeezing.

AVOCADO, ROCKET & GRAPEFRUIT SALAD
WITH SUNFLOWER SEEDS

This vibrant recipe is elegant, simple and classic. The addition of sunflower seeds and flaxseed oil boosts the omega-3 content and adds some texture.

**2 pink grapefruits, peeled and
    segmented**
2 ripe avocados, sliced
100 g/4 cups rocket/arugula

VINAIGRETTE
1 teaspoon clear honey
3 tablespoons champagne vinegar
4 tablespoons flaxseed/linseed oil
3 tablespoons sunflower seeds
**sea salt and freshly ground
    black pepper**

SERVES 4

For the vinaigrette, whisk the honey, champagne vinegar and flaxseed oil together in a mixing bowl, adding the sunflower seeds at the last minute so as not to damage them. Season to taste.

Place a layer of rocket on each plate. Arrange the grapefruit and avocado on top, with alternating slices of grapefruit and avocado in concentric semi-circles. You needn't arrange the fruit in this way if you're in a hurry, but it looks great when entertaining.

Lightly drizzle a line of vinaigrette horizontally across the half-moons of alternating grapefruit and avocado. Enjoy immediately.

CHAYOTE & GRAPEFRUIT SALAD

Chayote (or chow chow as it is sometimes known) is a member of the gourd family. It has a mild taste but this means that it happily absorbs and takes on the flavours of the lime, paprika and salt in this salad. The goal here is to cook it just enough to soften it but still leave it with a delightful crunch.

3 tablespoons pumpkin seeds
1 chayote (chow chow)
**1 pink grapefruit or orange, peeled
    and segmented**
**1 small bunch of coriander/cilantro,
    chopped**
1 tablespoon lime juice
2 tablespoons olive oil
¼ red onion, very thinly sliced
20 g/1 scant cup rocket/arugula
a pinch of paprika
a pinch of sea salt

SERVES 2

Put the pumpkin seeds in a dry frying pan/skillet over a low heat. Stir continuously for 7–10 minutes, taking care not to let them burn. Remove from the heat and set aside to cool.

Put the whole chayote in a saucepan and cover with water. Bring to the boil, then simmer for 10 minutes. Drain and set aside to cool slightly.

When the chayote has cooled, cut it in half, remove the stone/pit and cut each half into thin wedges.

Peel the grapefruit, remove the bitter white pith and cut the flesh into neat segments.

Mix all the ingredients together in a large bowl, the divide amongst plates and serve.

PEKING DUCK SALAD

The dark rich colour of the duck contrasts with the varying shades of green from the vegetables in this pretty salad. This is a quick, impressive and very satisfying dish, perfect when time is short and you have hungry mouths to feed.

2 duck breast fillets, skin on (approx. 160 g/5½ oz. each)
2 tablespoons hoisin sauce
1 tablespoon groundnut/peanut oil
2 tablespoons lime juice
1 small cucumber, thinly sliced, lengthways into ribbons
100 g/2½ small bunches pak choi/ bok choy, chopped
4 spring onions/scallions, thinly sliced
sea salt and freshly ground black pepper

SERVES 4

Brush the duck all over with half of the hoisin sauce.

Heat the groundnut oil in a frying pan/skillet. Add the duck, skin-side down, and cook for 5 minutes, or until the skin is crisp.

Turn the duck and cook for a further 5 minutes, or until cooked as desired.

Reserve the meat juices, to serve. Cover the duck, let it rest for 5 minutes and then slice thinly.

Whisk the lime juice and the meat juices in a large bowl. Add the duck, cucumber, pak choi and spring onions and mix. Season to taste and serve.

GRAPEFRUIT & PRAWN SALAD

This makes a lovely change from prawn cocktail! Buy the juiciest-looking cooked prawns you can find and leave them in the marinade for as long as possible. Pink grapefruit, used here, looks prettier and tastes sweeter than the white variety.

1 garlic clove, crushed
freshly squeezed juice of 1 lime
2 tablespoons sweet chilli/chili sauce
200 g/7 oz. cooked tiger prawns/ jumbo shrimp, peeled but tails left on
1 pink grapefruit
2 tablespoons extra virgin olive oil
100 g/1 cup cherry tomatoes, halved
1 small ripe avocado, diced
½ red onion, thinly sliced
a handful of coriander/cilantro

SERVES 2

Put the garlic, lime juice and sweet chilli sauce in a shallow, non-metallic container and whisk with a fork to combine. Add the prawns, stir to coat with the mixture, cover and set aside in a cool place to marinate whilst you prepare the rest of the salad.

Cut away the peel and pith from the grapefruit with a serrated knife. Hold the grapefruit in the palm of your hand and cut away each segment, working over a large bowl to catch the juices.

Add the olive oil to the grapefruit juice and whisk with a fork to combine. Add the grapefruit segments, cherry tomatoes, avocado, red onion and coriander to the bowl and toss to combine.

Divide the prepared salad between serving plates, or glasses for a cocktail effect. Remove the prawns from their marinade (using tongs or a slotted spoon) and arrange them on top. Drizzle the remaining marinade over the salad and serve at once.

LEMON, FENNEL & ROCKET SALAD
WITH RADICCHIO

Lemons grow profusely in the south of Italy and they're sweet enough to eat off the trees! Lemon can improve the flavour of any dish, whether it's a squeeze of the juice or a sprinkling of the zest. Here, however, lemon slices take centre stage, pulling together the aniseed notes of fennel, the peppery rocket and the bitter radicchio.

½ radicchio (red chicory), the leaves torn into large shreds

2 large unwaxed lemons, peeled and finely sliced

1 fennel bulb, peeled and finely sliced

a generous handful of rocket/ arugula, torn if the leaves are large

2 tablespoons extra virgin olive oil

2 tablespoons freshly grated Parmesan cheese

a few drops of good balsamic vinegar

sea salt and freshly ground black pepper

SERVES 4

Arrange the radicchio on 4 individual plates. Add the lemon slices, fennel and rocket.

To make the dressing, mix together the olive oil, Parmesan cheese and vinegar in a small bowl and season to taste with salt and pepper.

Pour the dressing over the plated salad just before serving.

SPICY & SWEET SALAD
WITH KUMQUATS & BRAZIL NUTS

The kumquat is a small, oval fruit with a strong and pleasant citrus smell. It grows on the coast and can be eaten whole, without peeling. The contrast of the sweet rind and the juicy, sour centre is quite special. It's a wonderful addition to salads and sure to be the topic of many a conversation during long and lazy summer dinners if you include this fruity salad in your repertoire! You can use orange juice instead of lemon juice, if you'd like to ring the changes with a different citrus fruit.

100 g/4 cups rocket/arugula
150 g/3 cups curly endive
10–15 kumquats, thinly sliced
    (or use seedless mandarin
    segments if you can't find
    kumquats)
60 g/½ cup Brazil nuts, chopped

DRESSING
2 tablespoons raw honey
    or agave nectar
1 tablespoon chilli/chili-infused
    olive oil
2 tablespoons chia seed oil
    or other oil
4 tablespoons freshly squeezed
    lemon juice
sea salt and freshly ground
    black pepper

SERVES 4

For the dressing, put the honey or agave nectar, olive oil, chia seed oil and lemon juice in a small jar, seal tightly and shake to emulsify.

Alternatively, put the ingredients in a small bowl and whisk gently to combine. Add a little water if needed. Season with salt and pepper to taste.

Put the rocket, endive, kumquats and Brazil nuts in a salad bowl and add the dressing. Mix gently, then serve immediately before the greens have time to wilt.

QUINOA & RED RICE SALAD
WITH CASHEW NUTS & CITRUS GINGER DRESSING

Quinoa is one of those slightly tricky grains that can be bland and soggy if under-seasoned and overcooked. Toasting the quinoa before boiling it in water gives it a lovely nutty flavour and helps it retain its texture.

2 red onions, cut into wedges,
   peeled but root intact
3 tablespoons olive oil
1 teaspoon brown sugar
60 g/⅔ cup cashew nuts
200 g/1¼ cups quinoa
200 g/1 cup Camargue red rice
100 g/⅔ cup raisins
2 handfuls of rocket/arugula
4 spring onions/scallions,
   thinly sliced
sea salt and freshly ground
   black pepper

DRESSING
5 tablespoons olive oil
1 tablespoon sesame oil
freshly squeezed juice and grated
   zest of 1 orange
1 tablespoon rice wine vinegar
a 5-cm/2-in piece of ginger, peeled
   and finely grated
1 long red chilli/chile, seeded
   and finely diced
1 garlic clove, finely grated

SERVES 6

Preheat the oven to 170°C (325°F) Gas 3.

Put the onion wedges on a baking sheet, drizzle with the olive oil, sprinkle with brown sugar and season with salt and pepper. Roast in the preheated oven for 25 minutes until meltingly soft. Remove from the oven and set aside to cool completely.

Meanwhile, scatter the cashew nuts on a separate baking sheet and toast in the same oven as the onion for 8 minutes. Remove from the oven and set aside to cool.

Once you have roasted the cashew nuts, spread the quinoa evenly on another baking sheet and toast in the same oven for 10 minutes.

Set 2 saucepans or pots filled with salted water over a medium heat and bring to the boil. Add the red rice to one pan and simmer for 20 minutes. Add the toasted quinoa to the other pan and simmer for 9 minutes. Once cooked, both should still have a little bite.

Drain off the water in both pans using a fine-mesh sieve/strainer. Transfer the quinoa and rice to a large mixing bowl. Set aside to cool.

To make the dressing, whisk all of the ingredients together in a small bowl to emulsify the oils with the orange juice and vinegar.

Pour the dressing into the bowl with the rice and quinoa. Add the roasted red onions, toasted cashew nuts, raisins, rocket and spring onions. Season with salt and pepper and serve.

POWERHOUSE SALAD

This amazing bowl of goodness is all you need to satisfy your hunger without feeling heavy afterwards. Walnuts, sunflower seeds and an avocado dressing are very filling and will give you plenty of energy; alfalfa sprouts, grapefruit and greens will add a touch of freshness and rehydrate your body; and olives will bring a salty and slightly bitter taste to this power bowl! It can be served as a side dish for dinner but it's so full of flavours and nutrients that it can hardly be deemed just another salad.

2 handfuls of rocket/arugula
a handful of baby spinach leaves
a handful of red radicchio
5 tablespoons sweetcorn
2 tablespoons alfalfa sprouts
1 red grapefruit, peeled and
    segmented
2 tablespoons pitted black olives,
    e.g. Kalamata or Niçoise
3 tablespoons walnut halves
1 tablespoon sunflower seeds
1 teaspoon chia seeds

DRESSING
1 ripe avocado
2 tablespoons umeboshi vinegar
freshly squeezed lemon juice,
    to taste
freshly ground black pepper

SERVES 2–3

Put the ingredients in a salad bowl and toss gently.

For the dressing, put the ingredients in a food processor and blend until smooth, adding a little water if needed. Season with black pepper.

Divide the salad amongst chilled bowls and drizzle the dressing on top just before serving.

GRILLED SQUID SALAD
WITH HERB-LIME DRESSING

This is such a pretty salad with the different layers yielding many different flavours, colours and textures. It is also delicious with prawns/shrimp. Use peeled green ones with the tail on and grill them the same way as the squid.

2 red (bell) peppers
800 g/1¾ lbs. cleaned squid
2 heads of chicory, leaves removed and cut in half lengthways
30 g/½ cup baby spinach leaves
40 g/¼ cup edamame or broad/fava beans (fresh or frozen), blanched

DRESSING
freshly squeezed juice of 2 limes
2 tablespoons olive oil
2 tablespoons palm sugar
1 garlic clove, grated
30 g/½ cup finely chopped coriander/cilantro, plus extra to garnish
15 g/¼ cup finely chopped basil
2 tablespoons fish sauce
1 long fresh red chilli/chile, seeded and finely chopped
freshly ground black pepper

a baking sheet, lined with foil

SERVES 4

Preheat the oven to 200°C (400°F) Gas 6.

Begin by roasting the red peppers. Place on the prepared baking sheet and roast in the preheated oven for 20 minutes. Turn and roast for a further 20 minutes until the peppers collapse and the skin is charred and soft.

Transfer to a small mixing bowl, cover with clingfilm/plastic wrap and set aside. When the peppers are cool enough to handle, remove and discard the skin and seeds, and slice the flesh.

To make the dressing, combine all the ingredients in a small mixing bowl using a whisk. It is important to make the dressing by hand rather than using a blender as you want the dressing to have texture.

To prepare the squid, cut off but reserve the tentacles and cut down the 'seam' of the squid so it opens out flat. Score the inside with a cross-hatch pattern, then slice lengthways into 2-cm/¾-inch wide strips. Cut the tentacles in half and add to the squid strips.

Preheat a frying pan/skillet over a medium–high heat. Sear the squid and the tentacles for 1–2 minutes until curled up and slightly charred. Remove the pan from the heat and dress with 2 tablespoons of the herb lime dressing.

Layer the chicory, spinach, sliced roast peppers and edamame on a platter. Drizzle with the remaining dressing, and gently mix through. Place the squid on top, garnish with extra coriander and serve.

3

MAIN DISHES

LEMON LAMB EN PAPILLOTE

Something of a Trojan horse… 'en papillote' is the French term for cooking food in a parcel of parchment or foil. In this instance, the paper is concealing Hellenic notes of lemon, oregano, sweet prunes and lamb neck fillets, slow cooked for a meltingly delicious gift-wrapped meal. This recipe serves two, but simply double up if you need a meal for four people. Goat or lamb neck fillets can be used (but they must be fillets, not neck with the bone).

60 g/⅓ cup dried yellow split peas
2 new potatoes, thinly sliced
4 small spring onions/scallions, whole
10 fine green/French beans, trimmed
3 soft, pitted prunes, halved
2 ripe tomatoes, thinly sliced
2 garlic cloves, chopped
125 ml/½ cup dry rosé or white wine
2 teaspoons Greek dried oregano
400 g/14 oz. lamb or goat neck fillet
60 ml/¼ cup passata (Italian strained tomatoes)
2 teaspoons butter
finely grated zest of 2 lemons, plus lemon wedges to serve
2 pinches of freshly chopped flat-leaf parsley
sea salt and freshly ground black pepper
olive oil, to drizzle
rustic bread, to serve

SERVES 2

Preheat the oven to 180°C (350°F) Gas 4.

Begin by cutting out 2 pieces each of foil and baking parchment, both about 45-cm/18-inches square. Lay out the sheets of foil and place the baking parchment on top (ready to fill and parcel up).

Drizzle a little olive oil in the middle of each square of baking parchment, pile half the yellow split peas in the centre of each parcel, followed by half the potato slices, half the spring onions (bent in half), half the fine beans, half the sliced prunes and half the sliced tomato, reserving a slice of tomato to put on top of the meat. Add 1 garlic clove to each one and then pour half the wine into each. Dust each with a pinch of the oregano and season with salt and pepper.

Season the lamb or goat neck fillets all over with salt and pepper and dust with the remaining oregano. Put them on top of the piles of vegetables and spoon half the passata over each one. Dot each with butter, sprinkle the zest of a lemon into each and finish with a pinch of chopped flat-leaf parsley.

Bring the sides of the baking parchment together to form packages, twist the ends so they are sealed and fold the tops over by 2.5 cm/1 inch. Bring up the edges of the underlying foil and hug it around the package, holding it all in place.

Cook in the preheated oven on a wire pizza rack on top of a baking sheet (to help the hot air circulate under the parcel) for 3 hours.

Once cooked, remove from the oven and let rest for at least 15 minutes, unopened, by which time the lamb or goat will be rested and tender.

Tip the contents of each parcel into a shallow serving bowl with some lemon wedges for squeezing. Serve with some rustic bread to mop up the juices.

SEVILLE LAMB RIBLETS

Lamb riblets are an underused part of the animal, which is a shame. Cooked until almost crisp, these bones are the mast to a sail of deliciously rich meat. These are prepared with a Seville orange marmalade sauce, which cuts through the richness, making a pile of them a delight to devour.

a 700-g/1½-lb. lamb rib (also known as belly lamb), bone-in, cut into riblets
2 tablespoons sherry vinegar
1 teaspoon cumin seeds
2 tablespoons olive oil
4 tablespoons Seville orange marmalade/preserve
2 tablespoons cider vinegar
2 tablespoons caster/granulated sugar
1 garlic clove, crushed
1 red chilli/chile, seeded and finely chopped (optional)
sea salt and freshly ground black pepper
a few sprigs of thyme, to garnish
finely grated orange zest, to garnish

SERVES 4

Put the riblets in a single layer in a non-reactive dish and pour over the sherry vinegar. Add the cumin seeds and season generously with salt and pepper, massaging everything together with your hands. Cover and marinate overnight in the fridge, or cook straight away if you can't wait!

Preheat the oven to 180°C (350°F) Gas 4.

Arrange the marinated riblets on a baking sheet with plenty of space amongst them, drizzle over the olive oil and bake, uncovered, in the preheated oven for 1½ hours until they are crisp around the edges.

To make the sauce, combine the marmalade, cider vinegar, sugar, garlic and chilli (if using) in a small saucepan and set over a medium heat. Bring to the boil and as soon as the mixture bubbles, reduce the heat to a simmer, cook for 2 further minutes, and then remove from the heat.

Spoon half the sauce onto a serving dish or board, pile the ribs on top and drizzle over the remaining sauce. Add a sprinkling of sea salt, and scatter over the thyme sprigs and orange zest to garnish. Serve with plenty of napkins for wiping sticky fingers and chins!

CAJUN CRISPY PORK BELLY
WITH KUMQUAT DIPPING SAUCE

There is nothing in the world better than crispy pork belly. The combination of earthy Cajun spices and the citrus of kumquats is light and bright. This is perfect as an appetizer on tossed salad greens, or it can be served on rice for a heartier course.

a 900-g/2-lb. pork belly,
   skin removed
2 bay leaves
60 ml/¼ cup white wine
1 teaspoon sea salt
1 teaspoon black peppercorns
vegetable oil, for searing

CAJUN SPICE RUB

2 teaspoons ground cumin
2 teaspoons cayenne pepper
2 tablespoons Spanish smoked
   paprika (pimentòn)
2 teaspoons dried thyme
2 teaspoons dried oregano
1 teaspoon dried garlic powder
2 teaspoons demerara/turbinado
   sugar
1 teaspoon sea salt
1 teaspoon ground black pepper

KUMQUAT DIPPING SAUCE

6 kumquats, thinly sliced
   (discard any seeds)
½ red Serrano chilli/chile,
   thinly sliced
120 ml/½ cup cider vinegar
2 tablespoons honey
1 teaspoon mirin (Japanese
   rice wine)

SERVES 4–6

Rinse the pork belly under cold water and pat dry with a paper towel. Put the pork in a lidded pan and add the bay leaves, white wine, salt and peppercorns. Pour in enough cold water to cover the pork by 5 cm/2 inches. Cover and bring to the boil over a medium–high heat, then reduce the heat and let the pork simmer for 1½ hours.

To make the kumquat dipping sauce, whisk all the ingredients together in a bowl, cover and put in the fridge until ready to use.

To make the Cajun spice rub, put all the ingredients in a bowl and mix together. Any excess that isn't used in this recipe can be stored in a glass jar with a tight-fitting lid for up to 6 months.

Remove the pork from the pan and place on large plate. Let it rest for 10 minutes, allowing it to cool enough to handle, then sprinkle 4 tablespoons of the Cajun spice rub over the pork and rub it in.

Slice the pork into 4-cm/1½-inch slices. Heat a cast-iron pan over a high heat until just smoking. Add a splash of vegetable oil, not too much, and sear the pork slices for 2 minutes on each side. Turn down the heat to medium–low and continue to cook for a further 4 minutes until crispy. The Cajun spices will blacken the pork.

Serve the pork with the cold dipping sauce.

PORK ESCALOPES
WITH LEMON SAUCE

Pork and chicken both work well with this lemon sauce, so you could always try it with bashed chicken breasts instead, if preferred. Serve with lemon wedges for squeezing.

4 pieces pork loin, 150-g/5 oz. each

100 g/2 cups sourdough breadcrumbs

grated zest and freshly squeezed juice of 2 lemons, plus lemon wedges, to serve

2 sprigs of rosemary, leaves picked and finely chopped

4 fresh sage leaves, finely chopped

100 ml/7 tablespoons milk

2 eggs

50 g/generous ⅓ cup '00' Italian flour or plain/all-purpose flour

100 g/7 tablespoons unsalted butter

2 tablespoons olive oil

120 ml/½ cup dry white wine

sea salt and freshly ground black pepper

SERVES 4

Cut off any excess fat from the pork, then wrap the slices in clingfilm/plastic wrap and bash with a rolling pin until they are about 5 mm/¼ inch thick.

Place the breadcrumbs in a bowl and add the grated lemon zest. Add the rosemary and sage and season with salt and pepper.

Mix the milk and eggs together in a bowl. Place the flour in a separate bowl, add a small pinch of salt and mix together.

Pat one of the pork escalopes in the flour. Next, dip the pork in the egg mixture, then coat in the breadcrumbs. Dip and coat the pork a second time so that it is really well covered in crumbs. Do the same with the rest of the pork.

Heat a large non-stick frying pan/skillet over a medium heat and melt half the butter with the olive oil. When the butter is foaming, add the escalopes and fry them for about 6 minutes on each side until golden brown. Drain on paper towels and keep warm.

To make the sauce add the remaining butter to a medium saucepan with the lemon juice and wine. Turn up the heat and let bubble until the sauce has reduced by half. Serve the pork with a wedge of lemon and the sauce on the side.

MEATBALLS IN AN EGG & LEMON SAUCE

Infinite in variety, meatballs in the form of 'kofta' or 'kibbeh' are part of an ancient Arab heritage and have remained as versatile food in street stalls, cafés, restaurants and in the home. Traditionally prepared with minced/ground beef, veal or lamb, the meat is pounded to a smooth texture with onions, spices and herbs, as well as ingredients such as nuts, dried fruits, breadcrumbs, rice and bulgur. They are then usually fried or grilled. The meatballs in this delicious version are cooked in a sauce which is bound with a liaison of egg and lemon – it's inspired by a traditional Turkish recipe and is packed with flavour and texture.

450 g/1 lb. finely minced/ground lean lamb
1 tablespoon medium or long-grain rice, washed and drained
a small bunch of dill, finely chopped
a small bunch of flat-leaf parsley, finely chopped
1–2 teaspoons sea salt
freshly ground black pepper
1–2 tablespoons plain/all-purpose flour
freshly chopped dill fronds, to garnish
fresh bread or cooked rice, to serve

SAUCE
2 carrots, peeled and diced
1 small celeriac/celery root, peeled, trimmed and diced (kept in water with a squeeze of lemon juice to prevent it discolouring)
2 potatoes, peeled and diced
2 egg yolks
freshly squeezed juice of 2 lemons
1 tablespoon labna, prepared overnight, or plain thick yogurt
1 teaspoon dried mint

SERVES 4–6

Put the lamb into a bowl with the rice, dill, parsley, salt and a good grinding of black pepper. Knead the mixture together for 5 minutes until thoroughly combined, and slap the mixture down into the bottom of the bowl to knock out the air – this is important to prevent the meatballs from coming apart when cooking in the liquid.

Take small portions of the mixture into the palm of your hand and mould them into tight, cherry-sized balls. Spoon the flour onto a flat surface and roll the balls in it until lightly coated. Put them aside.

For the sauce, pour 1 litre/4 cups water into a heavy-based, shallow saucepan and bring it to the boil. Drop in the carrots and celeriac, drained of the lemon water, and cook the vegetables for 5 minutes.

Keep the water boiling and drop in the meatballs. Reduce the heat, cover the saucepan and simmer for 15 minutes. Add the potatoes and simmer, uncovered, for a further 15–20 minutes until tender.

In a bowl, beat the egg yolks with the lemon juice, labna and dried mint. Spoon a little of the cooking liquid into the mixture, then tip it all into the pan, stirring all the time, until it is heated through and the sauce has thickened. Be careful not to bring the liquid to the boil as it will curdle.

Serve the meatballs straight from the saucepan into shallow bowls and spoon the sauce around them. Garnish with dill and serve with fresh bread or plain rice to mop up the sauce.

CABBAGE LEAVES
STUFFED WITH GOCHUJANG & LIME PORK

Gochujang is a fiery Korean chilli paste, which partners so well with the fragrant sweetness of lime. It is easy to find, either in grocery stores or online. These delicious appetizers are colourful, simple and packed full of flavour.

12 large Chinese cabbage or Savoy cabbage leaves
400 g/14 oz. minced/ground pork
2 tablespoons gochujang paste
grated zest of 3 limes, plus lime wedges, to serve
4 spring onions/scallions, thinly sliced
75 g/3 oz. fresh ginger, peeled and finely grated
2 garlic cloves, finely chopped
4 teaspoons tamari soy sauce
1 tablespoon toasted sesame oil
1 tablespoon Chinese rice vinegar
sea salt and freshly ground black pepper

CUCUMBER RELISH
1 cucumber
2 teaspoons clear honey
1 garlic clove, finely chopped
1 teaspoon tamari soy sauce
1 teaspoon toasted sesame oil
freshly squeezed juice of 1 lime
2 red chillies/chiles, finely chopped
sea salt and freshly ground black pepper

SERVES 4

Cut the tough ribs out of the leaves. Finely chop the ribs, place in a large bowl and set aside.

Submerge the whole leaves in boiling water for 3 minutes. Refresh in a bowl of ice-cold water, drain and pat dry with paper towel, then set aside.

Mix the minced pork with the gochujang paste, lime zest, spring onions, ginger, garlic, tamari soy sauce, toasted sesame oil and Chinese rice vinegar. Season with salt and pepper.

Divide the pork amongst between the leaves. Fold in the top and bottom and then lightly roll up to encase the filling. Place seam-side-down on a baking sheet as you finish each one.

Steam in batches in a steamer or metal sieve/strainer set over a pan of boiling water for 15 minutes until the pork inside is cooked through.

To make the cucumber relish, bash the cucumber with a rolling pin, then roughly chop and place in a bowl. Add the honey, garlic, tamari soy sauce, sesame oil, lime juice and chopped chillies and toss everything together. Season to taste with salt and black pepper.

Serve the parcels warm with the relish on the side for dipping and extra lime wedges to squeeze over.

BLACK BEAN RICE
WITH SLOW-COOKED PORK

This is a simple, satisfying rice dish bursting with Latin flavours of garlic, oregano and cumin, and a squeeze of orange. Perfect with the slow-cooked pork.

2 tablespoons olive oil
1 onion, finely chopped
1 garlic clove, finely chopped
200 g/1 cup long-grain white rice
700 ml/scant 3 cups chicken stock
    (stock cube is fine)
1 teaspoon dried oregano
1 teaspoon ground cumin
a pinch of dried chilli/hot red
    pepper flakes
freshly squeezed juice of ½ orange
1 x 400-g/14-oz. can black beans,
    drained and rinsed
30 g/1 oz. coriander/cilantro,
    plus extra to serve
grated zest and freshly squeezed
    juice of 2 limes, plus lime wedges,
    to serve
1½ tablespoons extra-virgin olive oil
sea salt and freshly ground
    black pepper
pickled jalapeños, to serve

SLOW-COOKED PORK
a 1.7-kg/3¾-lb. rolled pork
    shoulder/Boston butt, skin scored
1 onion, cut into wedges
2 tablespoons olive oil
1 tablespoon sea salt
1 tablespoon habanero chilli/
    chili sauce
1 tablespoon ground cumin
1 tablespoon instant coffee granules
1 tablespoon maple syrup
1 x 400-g/14-oz. can crushed
    tomatoes
500 ml/2 cups chicken stock
2 large ancho chillies/chiles,
    rehydrated
freshly squeezed juice of ½ orange
2 fresh bay leaves

SERVES 4

Preheat the oven to 220°C (425°F) Gas 7.

For the pork, place the pork shoulder in a deep-sided baking dish and tuck the onion wedges underneath it. Drizzle the pork skin with the olive oil, then massage the salt into the skin, forcing it into the score marks. Cook in the preheated oven for 30 minutes or until the crackling is crisp and golden.

In a bowl mix together the habanero chilli sauce, ground cumin, coffee and maple syrup, and rub all over the crackling. Then pour the canned tomatoes, chicken stock, ancho chillies and orange juice into the baking dish, add the bay leaves and place back into the oven. Turn the oven down to 180°C (350°F) Gas 4, and cook for 30 minutes per 500 g/1 lb. 2 oz., or until the pork is cooked through (the juices will run clear when the meat is pierced with a knife) – this will take about 2½–3 hours. Add more water if the sauce cooks down too much; it should be thick and rich.

Meanwhile, heat the olive oil in a saucepan over a medium–high heat, add the onion and garlic and sauté until tender. Add the rice, stir to coat, then add the stock, dried oregano, ground cumin, chilli flakes and orange juice, and season to taste. Bring to the boil, then reduce the heat to medium, cover with a tight-fitting lid and cook for 15–20 minutes until the rice is tender and liquid is absorbed.

Add the beans, coriander, lime juice and zest, and extra-virgin olive oil.

When the pork is cooked remove it from the baking dish and rest it for 20 minutes, covered, then shred the meat with 2 forks and mix in with the sauce.

Serve the rice hot with the pulled pork, topped with jalapeños and extra coriander, and with lime wedges alongside.

LEMON, BASIL & PEPPER WINGS

With three primary ingredients in this recipe, it's easy to mix and match and dabble with the flavouring. In any event, these wings are delicious in winter when citrus is in season, or in summertime when it gives a refreshing zing.

1.8 kg/4 lbs. chicken wings, halved at the joints, tips removed
2 tablespoons freshly ground black pepper
3 tablespoons freshly squeezed lemon juice
2 teaspoons seasoned salt
1½ teaspoons smoked paprika
1 teaspoon garlic powder
½ teaspoon dried chilli flakes/ hot red pepper flakes
2 tablespoons freshly chopped basil, plus a few whole leaves to serve
4 tablespoons olive oil
3 tablespoons grated lemon zest, plus lemon wedges, to serve

GARLIC-CREAM DIPPING SAUCE
120 g/½ cup plain yogurt
120 ml/½ cup sour cream
100 g/½ cup mayonnaise
8 garlic cloves, or to taste, finely chopped
¼ teaspoon paprika
½ teaspoon salt
¼ teaspoon freshly ground black pepper
snipped chives, to garnish

SERVES 4–6

Combine all the ingredients except the lemon zest in a large bowl. Toss until the wings are thoroughly coated. Cover the bowl with clingfilm/plastic wrap and marinate in the refrigerator overnight (or for at least 4 hours).

Mix all the ingredients for the dipping sauce together until smooth and well combined. Chill until ready to serve, then garnish with chives just before serving.

When ready to cook the wings, preheat the oven to 200°C (400°F) Gas 6.

Line 2–3 baking sheets with foil.

Arrange the wings on the baking sheets and pour the leftover marinade over them.

Bake for about 30 minutes, or until the wings are golden brown on each side and the juices run clear when the thickest part is pierced to the bone.

Remove the wings from the oven and let cool briefly. Sprinkle with the lemon zest and some basil leaves, and serve with the lemon wedges for squeezing over.

WHOLE POT-ROAST CHICKEN
WITH LEMON, OLIVES & SWEET SPICES

A whole roast chicken with Moroccan flavourings is delicious and slightly unusual. The skin on the breast is separated from the flesh underneath in order to make space for the rich buttery stuffing that melts into the bird. This keeps it beautifully moist, whilst adding a wonderful flavour. You can serve it with a side of roasted sweet potato fries or the more traditional couscous, or, if you like, serve with both.

a 1.75-kg/3¾-lb. chicken
4 sprigs each of rosemary and
    oregano, bashed
4 bay leaves, bashed
2 lemons
100 g/7 tablespoons unsalted
    butter, softened
50 g/½ cup pitted green olives,
    finely chopped
1 garlic clove, crushed
2-cm/¾-inch piece of fresh ginger,
    peeled and finely grated
½ teaspoon ground cinnamon
¼ teaspoon ground turmeric
½ teaspoon freshly ground black
    pepper
1 tablespoon clear honey
a handful of cilantro/coriander
    leaves
sea salt
couscous and/or sweet potato fries,
    to serve

SERVES 4

Preheat the oven to 200°C (400°F) Gas 6.

Place the chicken on a board and carefully slip your fingers under the skin at the neck end of the breast, separating it from the flesh. This will make a pocket for the butter mixture. Cut a couple of slashes into each thigh. Season the cavity of the chicken and pop half the rosemary and oregano, the bay leaves, and one lemon half inside.

Place the butter in a bowl and beat in the olives, garlic, ginger, spices, pepper, and some salt until evenly combined. Push as much of the butter up under the loosened skin as possible, spreading it flat. Spread the remaining butter over the legs and thighs of the chicken and down into the slashes. You can leave the chicken to marinate in the fridge for several hours at this stage, if liked.

Cut the remaining lemons into chunks and place in the base of an oval 5–6-litre/quart Dutch oven, along with the remaining rosemary and oregano, then place the chicken on top.

Cover the pan, transfer to the preheated oven, and cook for 30 minutes, then remove the lid and cook for a further 30 minutes until the chicken is golden and cooked through (pierce the thickest part of the chicken with the tip of a sharp knife and check the juices run clear). Remove the pan from the oven and transfer the chicken to a serving platter. Wrap in foil and rest for 10 minutes.

Using a slotted spoon, remove the herbs and lemons from the cooking juices. Tip the pan gently onto one side, then spoon away and discard as much of the fat as you can, leaving the chicken juices only.

Place the pan over a medium heat and stir in the honey until dissolved. Pour the juices over the chicken and scatter with the coriander.

Serve carved into portions with some couscous and/or roasted sweet potato fries.

HAWAIIAN SALMON SCRAPS
WITH GUAVA PONZU

A fish fry is a standard post-fishing activity in Hawai'i, where everyone comes together while the daily catch is fried in batches and served as it comes, along with a selection of dipping sauces and some citrus wedges, for all to enjoy. This particular recipe is for a fish fry with a fruity ponzu, but it is easily adaptable to personal preference and depending on both fish and fruit availability.

4 firm fish fillets, for frying
   (salmon belly works well)
mochiko rice flour (or cornflour/
   cornstarch), for dusting
vegetable oil, for frying
cooked rice, steamed greens
   and lime wedges, to serve

GUAVA PONZU SAUCE
4 tablespoons light soy sauce
3 tablespoons white vinegar
freshly squeezed juice of ½ lemon
1 teaspoon vegetable oil
3½ tablespoons tangy fruit juice
   of your choice, such as guava,
   yuzu or pineapple
freshly ground black pepper

SERVES 4

To make the guava ponzu, mix the soy sauce, vinegar, lemon juice, oil and pepper together in a bowl. Squeeze in the guava juice (or a similar amount of juice from the fruit of your choice). Set aside.

Roll the fish fillets in the mochiko flour (or cornflour). The moisture from the fish should be enough to make the flour stick.

Heat some vegetable oil in a frying pan/skillet until hot, ensuring the base of the pan is generously covered in oil so the fish doesn't stick and burn.

Fry the fish for a minute or two on each side, depending on the size of the fillets. You may need to cook the fish in batches, to avoid overcrowding the pan.

Remove the fish using a slotted spatula and set on a plate lined with paper towels to drain the oil.

Serve immediately on a bed of white rice with some steamed greens, the guava ponzu dipping sauce and lime wedges.

OVEN-ROASTED HAKE
ON CITRUSY GREENS

Hake is a deliciously sweet and clean-tasting white fish found throughout the Mediterranean and is also one of the UK's most sustainable. Unfortunately it doesn't make it onto kitchen tables as much as the so-called 'big five' (haddock, cod, tuna, salmon and prawns/shrimp) and it should! Here the roasted fish rests on top of crisp, lightly roasted green vegetables enveloped in a wine, butter and lemon dressing. It's simple, beautiful and, best of all, it's all cooked in the oven in one pan.

250 g/9 oz. on-the-vine cherry tomatoes
60 ml/¼ cup olive oil
200 g/7 oz. fine green/French beans, trimmed
3 garlic cloves, sliced
200 ml/¾ cup white wine
200 g/4 scant cups spinach leaves, washed and stemmed
200 g/7 oz. asparagus spears, trimmed
250 g/2 cups frozen petit pois
2 lemons, cut into quarters
60 g/½ stick butter
4 x 200-g/7-oz. hake fillets, skinned
2 tablespoons chopped flat-leaf parsley
2 tablespoons chopped dill
sea salt and freshly ground black pepper
boiled new potatoes, to serve (optional)

SERVES 4

Preheat the oven to 220°C (425°F) Gas 7.

Snip the vines of the cherry tomatoes with kitchen scissors to make four roughly even-sized pieces. Put them on a baking sheet, drizzle with a little of the olive oil and season with salt and pepper. Bake in the preheated oven for 10–12 minutes, just to warm them through and split the skins slightly. Set aside.

Put the beans and garlic in a large, deep-sided roasting pan. Pour over the wine and add a splash of the olive oil. Mix together and bake in the preheated oven for 10 minutes then remove.

Next add the spinach leaves and toss them with the beans so that they wilt slightly from the heat.

Follow with the asparagus and petit pois, and toss again to combine. Squeeze the juice from the lemon wedges over the vegetables and drop the wedges into the pan. Season generously with salt and pepper, drizzle over the remaining olive oil and dot half the butter over the vegetables.

Place the hake fillets on top of the vegetables, season with salt and pepper and put the remaining butter on the fish, putting a small piece on each one.

Return the pan to the hot oven and roast for a further 7–10 minutes, until the flesh flakes easily.

To serve, add the roasted tomatoes to the pan, scatter over the chopped parsley and dill, and take the whole pan to the table. Serve with boiled new potatoes, if liked.

FISH STEW
WITH TAMARIND, HILBEH & DRIED LIMES

This deliciously sour and spicy stew is commonly found in Jordan, Egypt and Yemen, where both the sweet and sour limes grow. Sour limes, 'limun baladi', are dried whole to impart a musty, tangy flavour to dishes, particularly fish stews and soups. The other flavours of this dish, which can be prepared with fish steaks or large prawns/shrimp, echo the history of trade between Arabs and Indians – tamarind, turmeric, fenugreek and fresh coriander. Hilbeh is a distinctive paste made with fenugreek seeds that have been soaked in water until they form a jelly-like coating, then pounded with garlic, chilli/chile and fresh coriander. Dried tamarind pulp, dried limes or powdered dried lime and hilbeh are available in Middle Eastern stores.

120 g/4 oz. dried tamarind pulp, soaked in 350 ml/1½ cups hot water for 20 minutes
1–2 tablespoons olive oil
1 kg/2¼ lb. fish steaks, such as sea bream, grouper or sea bass
1 onion, halved and sliced
3–4 garlic cloves, chopped
40 g/1½ oz. fresh ginger, peeled and chopped
2 teaspoons ground turmeric
2–3 dried limes, pierced twice with a skewer
1–2 teaspoons hilbeh paste
roughly 12 small new potatoes, peeled and left whole
1 x 400-g/14-oz. can plum tomatoes, drained of juice
2 teaspoons granulated or palm sugar
a bunch of coriander/cilantro, finely chopped
sea salt and freshly ground black pepper
cooked rice and lemon wedges, to serve

SERVES 4–6

Squeeze the tamarind pulp in your hand to separate the pulp from the seeds and stalks, then strain the pulp through a sieve/strainer. Reserve the strained liquid.

Heat the oil in a heavy-based pan and sear the fish steaks for 1–2 minutes on each side, then transfer them to a plate.

Stir the onion, garlic and ginger into the pan until they begin to colour. Add the turmeric, dried limes and hilbeh, then toss in the potatoes and cook for 2–3 minutes.

Stir in the tomatoes with the sugar, pour in the strained tamarind liquid and bring the liquid to the boil. Reduce the heat, cover the pan and simmer gently for about 15 minutes, until the potatoes are tender.

Season with salt and pepper to taste, then slip in the seared fish steaks. Cover the pan again and cook gently for about 10 minutes until the fish is cooked.

Stir in half the coriander, then use the rest to garnish the dish. Serve hot with rice and lemon wedges to squeeze over the fish.

CRAB, CHILLI & LEMON LINGUINE

This recipe is light, clean, fresh and super tasty. It sings with the bold flavours of chilli, lemon and fresh parsley, which provide the perfect backdrop for crabmeat.

200 g/7 oz. cooked picked white crabmeat (you can use half white crabmeat and half brown for a fuller crab flavour)

a handful of flat-leaf parsley, chopped

4 tablespoons extra virgin olive oil, plus extra if needed

grated zest and freshly squeezed juice of 1 lemon

2 garlic cloves, squashed, peeled and halved lengthways

1 red chilli/chile, seeded and finely chopped

200 g/7 oz. dried pasta or 160 g/ 6 oz. fresh pasta

sea salt and freshly ground black pepper

SERVES 2

Put a large pan of salted water on to boil for the pasta.

Meanwhile, to make the sauce, combine the remaining ingredients apart from the pasta in a bowl. This is a fairly loose sauce, therefore add extra olive oil if it is too dry, and season with salt and black pepper.

When the salted water is at a rolling boil, add the pasta and cook according to the pack instructions.

Drain the pasta, but keep a cup of the cooking water.

Tip the hot drained pasta back into the pan, add the crab mixture and a small splash of the retained pasta cooking water. Toss with gusto until creamy and well combined.

Remove the halved garlic cloves and serve immediately.

SEABASS WITH ROASTED RED PEPPER BUTTER, BASIL & BLACK OLIVES

A whole fish stuffed with lemon and homemade butter – cooked on the barbecue.

1 whole sea bass or sea bream,
   gutted, washed and fins trimmed
1 lemon, cut into wedges
a small bunch of basil, leaves picked
120 ml/½ cup white wine
12 black or kalamata olives
sea salt and freshly ground
   black pepper

RED PEPPER BUTTER
2 red (bell) peppers
25 g/2 tablespoons unsalted butter
1 garlic clove

SERVES 2–4

Preheat the oven to 180°C (350°F) Gas 4.

To make the red pepper butter, roast the peppers in the preheated oven for 35 minutes. Remove from the oven and skin and seed the peppers. Place the pepper flesh, butter and garlic in a food processor and blend together until you have a smooth paste.

Preheat the barbecue or griddle/grill to medium.

On both sides of the fish make vertical incisions to the bone and insert the lemon wedges.

Smear the red pepper butter all over the fish and place the basil leaves into the cavity.

Place the fish onto a double thickness, large sheet of foil. Lift the sides of the foil slightly to make a parcel. Add the wine and olives and season with salt and pepper. Seal the foil.

Cook for about 30 minutes on the preheated barbecue or griddle. Check if cooked by inserting a metal skewer into the fish through the foil. Serve.

VENTRESCA OF RED TUNA
WITH ORANGE SAUCE

This is a traditional Spanish recipe inspired by the originality and the quality of the ingredients available. In April and May the rich fat of the ventresca (tuna belly) works wonderfully with the acidity of orange, but this dish will taste good any time of the year with tuna steaks instead.

a 500-g/1 lb. 2-oz. ventresca of red tuna, cut into quarters

1 tablespoon coarsely ground almonds, lightly toasted (you will need 1 tablespoon more for the sauce so prepare a batch)

Spanish olive oil, for frying

orange slices, to serve

ORANGE SAUCE

1 tablespoon PX (Pedro Ximenez) sherry

1 teaspoon sherry vinegar

1 tablespoon coarsely ground almonds, lightly toasted

freshly squeezed juice of 2 large oranges

freshly squeezed juice of ½ lemon

1 teaspoon bitter orange marmalade

SERVES 4

For the sauce, pour the PX sherry and sherry vinegar into a small saucepan and heat over a medium heat for about 2 minutes until reduced to about ½ teaspoon, then set aside.

Place the toasted ground almonds in an electric blender together with the sherry reduction and the rest of the sauce ingredients, and blend to combine. Transfer the mixture to a small saucepan and reduce the sauce by one-third by simmering it over a medium heat.

Oil a frying pan/skillet with just a few drops of olive oil. When hot add the tuna pieces to the pan and pan-fry them 'al punto' for 1–2 minutes on each side, i.e. just sufficiently for the centre to be just cooked.

Serve individually plated with some orange sauce spooned over and around, with slices of orange and the toasted almonds scattered over the top.

MUSSELS WITH LEMON ZEST

Fresh mussels are available all year round, but from September to April they are at their best, and that is the ideal time to prepare this easy and original recipe.

1.5 kg/3¼ lb. fresh mussels,
    debearded and cleaned
3 tablespoons Spanish olive oil
1 white onion, thinly sliced
grated zest of 1 lemon
2 garlic cloves, chopped
200 ml/scant 1 cup dry white wine

SERVES 4

Heat the oil in a large deep-sided saucepan. Sauté the onion until soft but still white.

Add the garlic followed by the lemon zest. Cook for 2 minutes, add the mussels, stir and add the wine. Turn the heat up and cover the pan tightly.

Cook for 2–3 minutes until the mussels are open, shaking the pan a couple of times. The mussels should be plump and opaque; don't overcook them or they will shrivel.

Serve with the broth in which they have been cooked, discarding any mussels that have not opened.

MUSSELS WITH SAMPHIRE

The flavour and colour contrast in this recipe is glorious. Stringless green tips of samphire are best.

4 handfuls of samphire tips
200 ml/scant 1 cup dry white wine
2 small shallots, finely chopped
1 kg/2¼ lb. fresh mussels,
    debearded and cleaned
2 garlic cloves, crushed
a generous pinch of saffron
250 ml/1 cup sour cream
a generous handful of flat-leaf
    parsley, finely chopped
grated zest and freshly squeezed
    juice of 2 lemons
2 leeks, cut into matchsticks
2 small carrots, cut into matchsticks
sea salt and freshly ground
    black pepper
crusty bread, to serve

SERVES 4

Bring a pan of water to the boil and prepare a separate bowl of ice water. Add the samphire to the boiling water, cook for 1 minute or until tender, then plunge into the ice water.

Place the wine and chopped shallots in a pan and bring to the boil. Add the mussels and the garlic. Cover and leave for 3 minutes until the mussels are open. Discard any unopened mussels.

Remove all the mussels from the pot. Take the meat out of the shells, leaving 4 mussels in their shells. Put the meat back in the pan. Add the saffron, cream, parsley, lemon zest and juice. Season.

Place the samphire in the bowl with the reserved mussels in their shells. Spoon over the mussel broth, and leek and carrot. Serve with plenty of crusty bread to mop up the juices.

LEMON, MINT & CAPER SPAGHETTI

Things don't get much quicker than this. Very clean and simple,
it almost feels like you just ate a salad...

3 tablespoons extra virgin olive oil,
  plus extra if needed
a handful of mint leaves,
  roughly chopped
grated zest and freshly squeezed
  juice of ½ lemon
1 tablespoon capers, drained
  and rinsed
2 tablespoons pine nuts, toasted
200 g/7 oz. dried pasta or 160 g/
  6 oz. fresh pasta
sea salt and freshly ground
  black pepper
2 tablespoons finely grated
  Parmesan, to serve

SERVES 2

Put a large pan of salted water on to boil for the pasta.

Meanwhile, place the olive oil, chopped mint, lemon zest and juice, capers and pine nuts in the bottom of your serving bowl.

When the salted water is at a rolling boil, add the pasta and cook according to the instructions on the packet.

Drain the pasta but keep a cup of the cooking water.

Tip the hot drained pasta into the lemon caper mixture, and toss with gusto until the pasta looks creamy and well coated. If the pasta looks too dry, you can add a little more olive oil or a tiny splash of the retained pasta water and mix well.

Season to taste and serve immediately with the grated Parmesan and extra freshly ground black pepper.

SMOKED MACKEREL & PINK PEPPERCORN PASTA SALAD

The bold flavours in this fantastic dish are absolutely meant to be.

2 teaspoons pink peppercorns
a handful of flat-leaf parsley,
  finely chopped
½ teaspoon sea salt
¼ teaspoon freshly ground
  black pepper
4 tablespoons extra virgin olive oil,
  plus extra if needed
1 orange
freshly squeezed juice of ½ lemon
200 g/7 oz. smoked mackerel fillets
1 large fennel bulb, thinly sliced
a handful of dill, roughly chopped
200 g/7 oz. dried pasta or 160 g/
  6 oz. fresh pasta

SERVES 2

Grind the pink peppercorns, parsley, salt, black pepper and oil in a pestle and mortar until the peppercorns are crushed. Add the lemon juice to make a loose pesto-like dressing. Set aside.

Put a large pan of salted water on to boil for the pasta.

Meanwhile, zest the orange, then peel and segment it.

Flake the mackerel into a serving dish. Add the peppercorn dressing mixture, fennel, orange zest and segments and dill.

When the salted water is at a rolling boil, add the pasta and cook according to the instructions on the packet.

Drain the pasta, but keep a cup of the cooking water.

Tip the hot drained pasta into the mackerel mixture, add a splash of the pasta water and a little more olive oil if necessary. Toss with gusto until the pasta looks well coated and creamy.

Season to taste and serve.

LOBSTER TAILS
WITH LIME BUTTER

This is a recipe for a special occasion. Make friends with your fishmonger who can cut the tails in half for you.

5 tablespoons freshly squeezed lime juice
150 g/1¼ sticks unsalted butter
2 raw large lobster tails, cut in half
1 tablespoon olive oil
sea salt and freshly ground black pepper
2 limes, cut into wedges, to serve

SERVES 4

Preheat the oven to 200°C (400°F) Gas 6 and warm a baking sheet in the oven.

Heat the lime juice in a medium-sized saucepan. Add the butter and whisk to form a sauce.

Season the lobster tails. Heat the oil in a large frying pan/skillet and fry the lobster tails for 3 minutes.

Transfer them to the hot baking sheet, drizzle with lime butter and roast for 10 minutes until the flesh is opaque.

Serve with lime wedges for squeezing over.

THAI-STYLE KING PRAWNS

Fresh, vibrant and a winning combination of balanced flavours, this zingy dish makes a real crowd-pleaser as an appetizer.

2 tablespoons groundnut/ peanut oil
1 garlic clove, chopped
1 red chilli/chile, seeded and sliced
4 teaspoons finely chopped fresh ginger
400 ml/1⅔ cups chicken stock
2 tablespoons tamari soy sauce
a dash of Thai fish sauce
400 g/14 oz. raw king prawns/ jumbo shrimp, peeled and deveined

100 g/⅔ cup mangetout/ snowpeas, cut into strips
2 tablespoons freshly squeezed lime juice
a handful of coriander/cilantro leaves, chopped
4 spring onions/scallions, finely chopped
1 lime, cut into wedges, to serve

SERVES 4

Heat the oil in a wok or large, deep non-stick frying pan/skillet. Fry the garlic, chilli and ginger until they are starting to soften but still retain some bite; about 2 minutes.

Add the chicken stock, tamari soy sauce and fish sauce and bring to the boil.

Add the king prawns to the boiling stock and stir well. Add the mangetout and simmer for 3 minutes, or until the prawns are pink and cooked through. Remove from the heat and stir through the lime juice, fresh coriander and spring onions.

Serve immediately with wedges of lime for squeezing.

LIME, VEGETABLE & COCONUT CURRY

This delicious and easily made curry paste is vegetarian friendly as it doesn't contain dried shrimps or fish sauce. It helps if you have a food processor, or mini chopper, but you could also make the paste using a pestle and mortar. The vegetables don't need to be cooked for too long, otherwise they will lose their lovely vibrant colour and crispy texture. If you're using long-stemmed broccoli, opt for young, smaller stems.

2 x 400-ml/14-oz. cans full-fat coconut milk
100 ml/7 tablespoons well-flavoured vegetable stock
1 tablespoon demerara/turbinado sugar
100 g/3½ oz. cherry tomatoes, roughly chopped
1 yellow (bell) pepper, cut into strips
400 g/14 oz. mixed young vegetables (sugar snap peas, green/French beans, young, long-stem broccoli, baby corn, etc.)
a small bunch of fresh coriander/cilantro, roughly chopped
grated zest and freshly squeezed juice of 1 large lime

CURRY PASTE
45 g/1½ oz. fresh ginger, peeled
2 garlic cloves
1 stalk lemongrass, trimmed
3 kaffir lime leaves
1 tablespoon ground coriander
1 tablespoon ground cumin
1 scant tablespoon dried chilli flakes/hot red pepper flakes
1 tablespoon coconut oil
1–2 tablespoons warm water
a bunch of fresh coriander/cilantro

TO SERVE
a handful of cashew nuts
a bunch of spring onions/scallions, thinly sliced

SERVES 4

To make the curry paste, roughly chop the ginger, garlic and lemongrass and add them to a food processor or mini chopper and whiz until finely chopped (or bash them using a pestle and mortar if preferred). Add the lime leaves, ground coriander, cumin, chilli flakes and coconut oil. Pour in the warm water and blitz everything to a paste. Add the coriander and whiz again until everything is ground down and evenly mixed.

Preheat the oven to 180°C (350°F) Gas 4.

Pour the coconut milk and stock into a deep roasting pan and stir in the curry paste and sugar. Cover with foil and cook for 15 minutes.

Remove the pan from the oven, give everything a good stir and add the chopped tomatoes, pepper strips and prepared vegetables (cut the baby corn in half from top to bottom, if using). Replace the foil and cook for 10 minutes, or until the vegetables are just soft but retain their bright colours.

Stir in the fresh coriander and add the lime zest and juice. Serve straight away, scattered with cashews and spring onions.

SPRING VEGETABLES BARIGOULE
WITH ZINGY GREMOLATA

Just-cooked baby spring vegetables grow together and go together to create such a stunning dish and the zingy-fresh gremolata topping makes it super-special. Please take care not to overcook the vegetables though, because the pleasure is in the bright, vibrant flavours and colours, and it doesn't take too long to overcook them and lose both.

freshly squeezed juice of 1 lemon
    (use the zest for the gremolata)
2 globe artichokes
2 fennel bulbs
3 tablespoons olive oil
250 ml/1 cup white wine
1.25 litres/5 cups good-quality
    vegetable stock
1 fresh bay leaf
a few sprigs of tarragon
300 g/10½ oz. baby carrots
250 g/9 oz. radishes
250 g/generous 1½ cups fresh peas
450 g/1 lb. asparagus, trimmed
125 g/4 oz. tenderstem broccoli/
    broccolini or purple sprouting
    broccoli, trimmed

DRESSING
4 tablespoons brown rice syrup
4 tablespoons extra virgin olive oil
freshly squeezed juice of 1 lemon
    (use the zest for the gremolata)

GREMOLATA
finely grated zest of 2 lemons
a bunch of parsley, chopped
1 garlic clove, finely chopped

SERVES 4

Preheat the oven to 200°C (400°F) Gas 6.

Fill a bowl with cold water and add the lemon juice. Snap off the woody outside leaves of the artichokes and cut off the stems and tough tops. Cut them in half and remove the fluffy centres with a teaspoon. Cut each half into three and plunge them immediately into the acidulated water, to stop them from turning brown.

Trim the fennel bulbs, and cut them into wedges. Arrange them in a large, deep roasting pan and drizzle with the oil. Cook for 15 minutes, until they are starting to turn golden. Remove from the oven and pour in the white wine and stock. Add the bay leaf, tarragon sprigs, baby carrots and radishes to the pan. Take a piece of baking parchment and lay it over the liquid (much like you would use a cartouche if you were cooking on the hob/stovetop) and cook for about 10 minutes more until the carrots are just starting to soften.

Remove from the oven, take away the cartouche and add the fresh peas, asparagus and broccoli stems. Cover with the parchment and return to the oven for a further 5 minutes until the vegetables are just cooked and still have their lovely bright colour. Immediately drain away the stock, and reserve it for something else.

In the meantime, whisk all the ingredients for the dressing together in a bowl.

For the gremolata, mix the lemon zest, chopped parsley and garlic together in a separate bowl.

Serve the vegetables warm, drizzled with the dressing and scattered with the gremolata.

CYPRIOT FUL MEDAMES
WITH PRESERVED LEMON SALSA

This dish of spiced, crushed beans takes its inspiration from the Egyptian dish Ful Medames, but it has a Cypriot twist with cooling Greek yogurt and a sour-sweet salsa made from preserved lemons.

½ tablespoon cumin seeds
a splash of olive oil
1 red onion, diced
1 garlic clove, crushed
¼ teaspoon cayenne pepper
a cinnamon stick
1 large ripe tomato, diced
1 x 400-g/14-oz. can borlotti beans, drained and rinsed
160 ml/⅔ cup vegetable stock
a pinch of sugar
sea salt and freshly ground black pepper
dried chilli flakes/hot red pepper flakes, to garnish (optional)
a few coriander/cilantro leaves, to garnish
extra virgin olive oil, to drizzle
a few pinches of toasted sesame seeds
Greek yogurt and warmed pita breads, to serve

PRESERVED LEMON SALSA
1 tomato, seeded and diced
1 tablespoon diced red onion
½ preserved lemon, diced
2 tablespoons extra virgin olive oil, or to taste
1 tablespoon white wine vinegar, or to taste
1 tablespoon freshly chopped coriander/cilantro
sea salt

SERVES 2

To make the salsa, mix all the ingredients together in a small bowl and season with salt. Taste and add more extra virgin olive oil, vinegar or salt to taste. Set aside.

Toast the cumin seeds in a small, dry frying pan/skillet until just fragrant and tip into a mortar with ½ teaspoon of salt. Coarsely grind with a pestle and set aside.

Add a splash of olive oil to a large saucepan and fry/sauté the diced red onion for a few minutes until it has softened and started to caramelize. Add the garlic, ground cumin seeds, cayenne pepper and cinnamon stick. Before the spices start to catch, add the tomato and let simmer for 1 minute. Season generously with salt and pepper.

Add the borlotti beans, hot stock and sugar to the pan. Leave uncovered over low heat and on a gentle simmer for about 5 minutes, until the liquid has reduced by half.

Remove from the heat, discard the cinnamon stick and mash about half of the beans with a fork to get the mixture as smooth as possible – it will be a bit lumpy but you want texture so that's okay, just add a small splash of water if it's too thick.

Assemble the dish by spreading the warm bean mixture out on a serving plates and add a couple of tablespoonfuls of the preserved lemon salsa. Finish with a drizzle of extra virgin olive oil, a sprinkle of toasted sesame seeds, a pinch of dried chilli flakes (if using) and some torn coriander leaves.

Serve with dollops of Greek yogurt and warmed pita breads.

LEMON SPAGHETTI

This is a lovely summer dish, simple and fresh.

120 g/1 stick butter
finely grated zest of 1 lemon
  and freshly squeezed juice
  of 1½ lemons
200 g/7 oz. dried pasta or 160 g/
  6 oz. fresh pasta
a handful of basil leaves,
  roughly torn
sea salt and freshly ground
  black pepper
crumbled goat's cheese, to serve

SERVES 2

Put a large pan of salted water on to boil for the pasta.

Meanwhile, to make the sauce, heat the butter, lemon zest and lemon juice in a heavy-bottomed pan. When the butter begins to froth, remove the pan from the heat; do not allow it to burn.

When the salted water is at a rolling boil, add the pasta and cook according to the instructions on the packet.

Drain the pasta, but keep a cup of the cooking water.

Tip the hot drained pasta into the lemony butter, add the torn basil leaves and about 60 ml/¼ cup of the retained cooking water. Toss with gusto over a high heat until creamy and well coated.

Season to taste, top with crumbled goat's cheese and serve immediately with extra freshly ground black pepper.

ARTICHOKE, LEMON & PARMESAN PENNE

For those of you familiar with the iconic global dipping sensation, you will know that this artichoke heart, mayo and Parmesan combination is usually topped with more Parmesan and baked in the oven. Here it is deconstructed for a quick and surprisingly good hot pasta. If you don't like the idea of mayonnaise, you can replace it with a good glug of extra virgin olive oil or some crème fraîche.

2 heaped tablespoons good-quality
  mayonnaise
150 g/5½ oz. jarred artichoke
  hearts, drained and very roughly
  chopped
2 tablespoons finely grated
  Parmesan, plus extra to serve
grated zest of ½ lemon
200 g/7 oz. dried pasta or 160 g/
  6 oz. fresh pasta
sea salt and freshly ground
  black pepper

SERVES 2

Put a large pan of salted water on to boil for the pasta.

Meanwhile, to make the sauce, combine all the ingredients apart from the pasta in a cold pan off the heat.

When the salted water is at a rolling boil, add the pasta and cook according to the instructions on the packet.

Drain the pasta, but keep a cup of the cooking water.

Tip the hot drained pasta into the artichoke mayo mixture. Add a small splash of the retained pasta water and then toss with gusto over a high heat until the pasta looks creamy and well coated.

Serve immediately with extra grated Parmesan and extra freshly ground black pepper.

CARAMELIZED FENNEL & HERITAGE CARROTS

WITH ORANGES & LEMONY HERB DRESSING

Warm, caramelized fennel and colourful Heritage carrots make magnificent bedfellows to thin slices of fresh juicy oranges. Don't skimp on the herbs.

2 bulbs Florence fennel
600 g/21 oz. Heritage carrots
4–5 tablespoons olive oil
freshly squeezed juice of 1 lemon
2 teaspoons caster/granulated
    sugar
4 juicy oranges
sea salt and freshly ground
    black pepper

DRESSING
100 ml/7 tablespoons olive oil
grated zest and freshly squeezed
    juice of 1 lemon
1 teaspoon caster/granulated sugar
a large handful of chopped mixed
    herbs (parsley, coriander/cilantro,
    dill, chives, etc.)

SERVES 4

Preheat the oven to 190°C (375°F) Gas 5.

Trim the fennel bulbs, and then cut them in half, from root to tip. Cut each half into three or four wedges. Arrange on a baking sheet. Cut the carrots in half or into quarters along their length, depending on the size of the carrots. Arrange them on the baking sheet with the fennel wedges. Drizzle over the oil and lemon juice and scatter over the sugar. Roast for 25–30 minutes until the vegetables are soft and slightly charred at the edges.

In the meantime, top, tail and peel the oranges and cut into thin slices.

Mix the oil, lemon juice and sugar together for the dressing, and squeeze in any juice from the end pieces of orange peel. Season with a little salt and black pepper.

Remove the pan from the oven and transfer everything to a platter. Drizzle over the lemon dressing, scatter with the herbs, and serve.

4

SWEET THINGS

CITRUS FRUITS
WITH LAVENDER HONEY

Around the world lavender is used in so many products; from soaps and shampoos, to chocolate and herbal remedies. It is actually a member of the mint family and a close relation of rosemary, sage and thyme – and it pairs perfectly with citrus fruits.

2 sweet oranges
2 blood oranges
2 seedless mandarins
1 white grapefruit
8 kumquats
120 g/⅓ cup lavender honey
    (or lavender-infused honey)
freshly squeezed lemon juice,
    to taste
½ teaspoon dried lavender buds

SERVES 4

Peel the oranges, mandarins and grapefruit and separate into segments. Very thinly slice the kumquats.

If your honey has crystallized, place the jar in warm water for 10 minutes to soften.

Divide all the fruit amongst 4 plates, drizzle the honey and lemon juice, to taste, over the top and finish with lavender flowers.

This is such a fragrant dessert – and it is so elegant and refined, and yet so simple!

ORANGE-BAKED RHUBARB

Rhubarb and orange are delightful together and make for a fine dish when baked. Rhubarb has a finite season so make the most of it whilst it is around. The flavours here work exceedingly well with something creamy alongside, such as creamy Greek yogurt or coconut milk yogurt.

400 g/14 oz. rhubarb, rinsed and
    cut into 5-cm/2-inch pieces
grated zest and freshly squeezed
    juice of 1 orange
1½ tablespoons honey
yogurt, to serve

SERVES 4

Preheat the oven to 180°C (350°F) Gas 4.

Put the rhubarb in a roasting pan. Squeeze over the orange juice and add the zest, then drizzle over the honey and stir everything together.

Bake in the preheated oven for 30 minutes until the rhubarb is soft, stirring once or twice during the baking time.

Serve with a generous dollop of your favourite yogurt.

CLEMENTINE & PISTACHIO CAKES

These clementine cakes add a certain wow to the tea table with their flurry of gold leaf and candied peel. Individual kugelhopf pans, used here, are available online or in good kitchenware stores.

2 clementines
100 g/⅔ cup shelled, unsalted
   pistachios
75 g/¾ cup ground almonds
100 g/¾ cup plain/all-purpose flour
1½ teaspoons baking powder
½ teaspoon ground cinnamon
a pinch of salt
3 large/US extra-large eggs
150 g/¾ cup caster/superfine sugar
3 tablespoons icing/confectioners'
   sugar
edible gold leaf

CANDIED CLEMENTINE PEEL
2 clementines
100 g/½ cup caster/superfine
   sugar, plus extra to sprinkle

SPICED CITRUS SYRUP
freshly squeezed juice of 1 lemon
100 g/½ cup caster/superfine sugar
1 cinnamon stick
4 cardamom pods, bruised
2 star anise

six 10-cm/4-inch kugelhopf pans,
   chilled, brushed with melted
   butter and dusted with flour

MAKES 6

You will need to make the candied peel the day before. Wash the clementines. Squeeze the juice, cover and reserve. Using a teaspoon, carefully scrape out any tough membrane from the inside of the clementine shells. Cut the peel into slices, 5 mm/½ inch thick. Bring a small pan of water to the boil, add the peel and simmer for 2 minutes. Drain and repeat twice more, boiling with fresh water.

Put the sugar into the cleaned-out pan, add 100 ml/7 tablespoons water and bring slowly to the boil to dissolve the sugar. Add the clementine peel and simmer for 30–40 minutes until tender and translucent. Using a slotted spoon, remove the peel from the syrup and arrange on a wire rack. Leave to dry overnight.

The next day, toss the dried peel in a little extra caster sugar and store in an airtight container.

To make the cake, wash the clementines, place in a small saucepan, cover with cold water and bring to the boil. Simmer gently for about 45 minutes, or until really tender. Drain and let cool.

Preheat the oven to 180°C (350°F) Gas 4.

Whiz the pistachios in a food processor until fine. Add the almonds, flour, baking powder, cinnamon and salt, and whiz for 10 seconds. Tip into a bowl.

Cut the cooked clementines in half and scoop out any pips. Roughly chop the fruit (skin and all), tip into the food processor and whiz until almost smooth.

Whisk the eggs and sugar in a stand mixer on high speed until very thick and pale. Fold in the clementine purée using a large metal spoon. Sift in the dry ingredients. Divide the batter amongst the kugelhopf pans and place them on a baking sheet. Bake on the middle shelf of the preheated oven for 30 minutes, or until well risen and golden.

For the spiced citrus syrup, pour half the reserved clementine juice into a small pan, add the remaining ingredients and bring slowly to the boil to dissolve the sugar. Simmer for 2–3 minutes, or until reduced by one-third. Let cool.

Let the cakes cool in the pans for 2 minutes, then turn out onto a wire rack, brush the syrup over them and let cool completely.

Whisk together the remaining clementine juice and just enough of the icing sugar to make a runny icing. Spoon over each cake. Let set for 5 minutes, then decorate with gold leaf and candied peel.

ROSEWATER, PISTACHIO & GRAPEFRUIT CAKE

Grapefruit is underused in cakes, but it makes a lovely change from oranges and lemons. You can buy crystallized pink rose petals in jars, or, to make your own, dip unsprayed petals in lightly beaten egg white followed by granulated sugar. Shake off the excess sugar, then leave the petals to dry on baking parchment until crisp.

200 g/1⅓ cups shelled, unsalted pistachios
200 g/1½ cups self-raising/self-rising flour
1 tablespoon bicarbonate of soda/baking soda
150 g/1¼ sticks butter, softened and cubed
150 g/¾ cup caster/superfine sugar
3 large/US extra-large eggs, lightly beaten
2 tablespoons rosewater
4 tablespoons buttermilk
grated zest of 2 pink or red grapefruit
crystallized rose petals, to decorate
Greek yogurt, to serve

GRAPEFRUIT SYRUP
1 pink or red grapefruit
1 tablespoon rosewater
75 g/6 tablespoons caster/superfine sugar

a 23-cm/9-inch springform cake pan, 6 cm/2¼ inch deep, lightly buttered

SERVES 10–12

Preheat the oven to 180°C (350°F) Gas 4.

Begin by whizzing 150 g/1 cup of the pistachios in a food processor until finely ground. Roughly chop the remaining 50 g/⅓ cup and mix three-quarters of them with the ground pistachios. Reserve the rest for decorating the cake.

Sift the flour and bicarbonate of soda into the bowl of an electric mixer. Add the butter and mix together, on the lowest speed, until the mixture resembles clumpy breadcrumbs. Add the pistachios, sugar, beaten eggs, rosewater, buttermilk and grapefruit zest and mix until combined. The mixture will be thick, so you will probably need to stop a couple of times to scrape the mixture off the paddle.

Tip the mixture into the prepared cake pan and spread it evenly with a spatula. Bake in the preheated oven for about 45 minutes, or until golden and risen.

Towards the end of the cooking time, make the grapefruit syrup. Squeeze the juice of the grapefruit through a sieve/strainer and into a medium pan. Add the rosewater and sugar to the pan and gently heat together, stirring, until the sugar has dissolved. Increase the heat and boil for 2 minutes to make the liquid slightly more syrupy.

When the cake is ready, remove it from the oven and, using a small, fine skewer, make a few holes over the surface of the cake. Spoon over the warm grapefruit syrup, allowing it to seep in between spoonfuls. Leave the cake to cool completely in its pan.

Once cold, pop the cake out of the pan and scatter the reserved chopped pistachios and a few crystallized rose petals on top. Serve with Greek yogurt.

LEMON, CARDAMOM & RASPBERRY TORTE

Proof that flourless cakes are divine – and work wonderfully with tangy lemon. Blueberries work as well as raspberries here. Serve this cake at the end of dinner parties with dessert wine for a memorable ending to any meal.

125 g/1⅛ sticks unsalted butter, plus extra for greasing
200 g/1 cup golden caster/granulated sugar
10 cardamom pods, seeds crushed
finely grated zest of 1 lemon
2 teaspoons pure vanilla extract
3 large/US extra-large eggs
200 g/1 cup raspberries or blueberries
250 g/1½ cups ground almonds
a pinch of salt
1 teaspoon baking powder (gluten-free, if needed)
chopped toasted hazelnuts, to decorate

ICING
grated zest and freshly squeezed juice of 1 small lemon
200 g/1½ cups icing/confectioners' sugar

a 23-cm/9-inch springform cake pan, greased and lined

SERVES 6–8

Preheat the oven to 170°C (325°F) Gas 3.

Cream together the butter, sugar, cardamom seeds, lemon zest and vanilla extract until pale and fluffy. Add the eggs one at a time and beat between each addition.

Fold in the fruit, ground almonds, salt and baking powder.

Fill the cake pan with the mixture and bake in the preheated oven for about 45 minutes until golden, and a skewer inserted into the centre comes out cleanly.

Allow to cool in the cake pan on a wire rack and then remove from the pan.

To make the icing, mix the lemon zest and juice with the icing sugar.

Pour the icing over the cooled cake and sprinkle with toasted hazelnuts to decorate.

ORANGE CREAM ROULADE

Roulades, or rolled sponge cakes, can be prepared with different types of sweet or savoury fillings, but zesty orange cream is a real crowd-pleaser. Serve it with some ice cream or whipped cream for a decadent dessert.

3 large/US extra-large eggs, separated
80 g/⅓ cup white caster/superfine sugar
80 g/⅔ cup plain/all-purpose flour
seeds from ½ vanilla pod/bean, split lengthways
finely grated zest and freshly squeezed juice of ½ orange

FILLING
175 g/6 oz. full-fat cream cheese
80 g/⅓ cup condensed milk
100 g/scant ½ cup double/heavy cream
freshly squeezed juice of ½ orange

TO FINISH
finely grated zest of ½ orange
icing/confectioners' sugar, to dust

30 x 45-cm/12 x 18-inch baking pan greased and lined with baking paper, plus a second piece of baking paper, the same size as the baking pan

SERVES 6

Preheat the oven to 190°C (375°F) Gas 5.

Place the egg whites in a bowl and use an electric hand whisk to start working the egg whites to peaks.

Halfway through, start adding the sugar, little by little, and continue to mix to a meringue consistency.

Use a spatula to carefully fold in the egg yolks, one by one, followed by the flour, vanilla and orange zest and juice. Pour into the prepared baking pan and use the spatula to level the surface.

Bake in the preheated oven for about 15 minutes, making certain the batter has been cooked completely. Leave it to cool down before removing from the pan.

While the batter is baking, start preparing the filling. Whisk the cream cheese, condensed milk, double cream and orange juice to a creamy texture.

Place the second piece of baking paper on top of the cooled roulade base. Carefully turn over and gently peel off the bottom layer of baking paper (which is now on top).

Pour the filling mixture over the base and use a spatula to spread over the whole surface. Use the baking paper underneath to start rolling the base as tightly as possible until it becomes a perfect roll. By then the paper will be in your hands.

Place the roulade in a rectangular serving dish and sprinkle with icing sugar and orange zest to finish.

Serve as soon as possible (the roulade should not be placed in the fridge to chill).

KEY LIME PIE

Everyone has their favourite version of this true classic, and this one is sure to please with its oaty base and zingy lime filling.

12 oat cookies, approximately 300 g/10½ oz.
150 g/1¼ sticks unsalted butter, melted
2 large/US extra-large egg yolks
1 x 397-g/14-oz can condensed milk
1 teaspoon sea salt
finely grated zest and freshly squeezed juice of 4 limes, plus extra grated zest to decorate
250 ml/1 cup double/heavy cream

a 23-cm/9-inch loose-based tart pan

SERVES 6–8

Preheat the oven to 160°C (325°F) Gas 3.

Crush the cookies to a fine crumb and mix with the melted butter. Pour into the tart pan and press evenly up the sides and base. Chill in the refrigerator for 30 minutes.

Once chilled, transfer the pan to the preheated oven and bake for 12 minutes. Cool on a wire rack.

Place the egg yolks in a large bowl and mix well. Add the condensed milk and continue mixing. Add the salt, lime zest and juice, and mix thoroughly. Pour into the cooled base and bake for 20 minutes.

Cover and chill for at least 4 hours.

To serve, whip the cream and pile on top of the lime filling, then sprinkle with extra lime zest.

COCONUT & SEMOLINA CAKE
WITH CITRUS SYRUP

This simple cake is made all over Greece with a few variations. It is really lovely with a mix of semolina and coconut and drenched with a citrus syrup, making for a moist cake that is great served with Greek yogurt.

100 g/1⅓ cups grated desiccated/ dried unsweetened shredded coconut
5 eggs, separated
220 g/generous 1 cup caster/ superfine sugar
300 g/2 cups coarse semolina or polenta/cornmeal
180 ml/¾ cup hot water
260 g/9½ oz. Greek-style yogurt, plus extra to serve
finely grated zest of ½ lemon
finely grated zest of ½ orange
80 g/¾ stick butter, melted

CITRUS SYRUP
300 g/1½ cups caster/superfine sugar
freshly squeezed juice and thinly peeled rind of 1 lemon and 1 orange

a 23-cm/9-inch square cake pan, greased, floured and lined

SERVES 6

Preheat the oven to 160°C (325°F) gas 3.

Scatter the coconut on a baking sheet and roast in the preheated oven for 5–10 minutes until golden. Set aside until needed.

Beat the egg yolks and half the sugar in an electric mixer for about 5 minutes until pale. Combine the semolina and hot water in a bowl, stir through the yogurt and lemon and orange zests and add to the yolk mixture. Beat to combine, leave to rest for 5–10 minutes, then stir through the melted butter.

Whisk the egg whites with a pinch of the sugar in an electric mixer until soft peaks form. Whisking continuously, gradually add the remaining sugar and whisk until the mixture is smooth and glossy. Fold this into the semolina mixture until combined.

Pour into the prepared cake pan, smooth the top and bake in the preheated oven for 45–60 minutes until golden and the centre springs back when lightly touched.

Cool in the pan for 20 minutes, then turn out onto a platter and pierce all over with a skewer.

Meanwhile, make the citrus syrup. Bring the sugar, lemon and orange juices and peel and 175 ml/¾ cup water to the boil in a saucepan, stirring to dissolve the sugar.

Ladle the syrup over the cake and leave to stand for 10–15 minutes until the syrup is absorbed.

Scatter over the roasted coconut and serve with extra yogurt.

CITRUS SALAD
WITH ROSEWATER CARAMEL

This is beautiful dish would be equally at home as a dessert or part of a summery brunch – colourful slices of citrus fruits drenched in a fragrant rosewater caramel syrup and topped with crunchy pistachios and dark chocolate shavings. The red grapefruit adds a bitter sharpness, but you can leave it out, if preferred.

2 blood oranges

2 oranges

1 red or pink grapefruit (optional)

2 kiwi fruit, gold if you can find these

12 small mint leaves

40 g/scant ⅓ cup shelled, unsalted pistachios, lightly crushed

1 tablespoon dried edible rose petals, lightly crushed

a 40-g/1½-oz. bar of dark/ bittersweet chocolate, chilled

thick Greek yogurt, to serve

ROSEWATER CARAMEL SYRUP

150 ml/⅔ cup warm water

200 g/1 cup caster/superfine sugar

1 cinnamon stick

30 g/2 tablespoons butter

a small pinch of salt

1 tablespoon rosewater

SERVES 6

Top and tail all the fruit and then hold each piece, one of the cut sides down, on a flat surface and use a sharp knife to slice away all the peel and pith (or kiwi skin) from the outside to reveal the flesh. Turn each piece on its side and cut the fruit into thin (just under 5-mm/¼-inch) slices. Arrange the slices on a large, flat platter.

To make the rosewater syrup, put half the warm water in a small saucepan with the sugar and cinnamon stick and set over a very low heat. Stir gently until the sugar has dissolved, then turn up the heat and stop stirring (you don't want it to start to crystallizing). Swirl the pan as it turns a blonde colour and starts to caramelize (this will take about 5 minutes).

At this point, take the pan off the heat and beat in the butter, rapidly followed by the remaining water. Keep beating until both are fully incorporated, then add the salt and return the pan to a very low heat. Bring to a simmer and simmer for 2 minutes, then remove from the heat and, once it's stopped bubbling, stir in the rosewater. Discard the cinnamon stick.

Pour the warm syrup over the prepared fruit platter, scatter over the mint leaves, pistachios and rose petals, and use a vegetable peeler to shave a little chocolate on top.

Serve with thick Greek yogurt on the side.

LEMON YOGURT SQUARES

These luscious zingy-light lemon squares are absolute winners...BUT...you must resist the urge to replace the full-fat Greek yogurt with a low-fat or 0% concoction, because, without the teeniest, tiniest shred of a doubt, the recipe simply won't be the same. Baking relies on accuracy much more than any other form of cooking. The flavour and consistency of a lower fat yogurt would really spoil the recipe and would also save very little in the way of calories.

125 g/½ cup plus 1 tablespoon
   butter, softened
200 g/1½ cups plain/
   all-purpose flour
50 g/¼ cup caster/superfine sugar

TOPPING
500 g/1 lb. 2 oz. full-fat Greek
   yogurt
300 g/1½ cups caster/superfine
   sugar
grated zest of 2 lemons
freshly squeezed juice of 4 lemons
4 eggs
2 egg yolks
80 g/⅔ cup plain/all-purpose flour

*a 30 x 17 x 2.5-cm/11¾ x 6¾ x
   1-inch brownie pan, lightly
   greased and lined with baking
   parchment*

MAKES 15

Preheat the oven to 180°C (350°F) Gas 4.

Rub the butter, flour and sugar together until the butter is evenly incorporated and the mixture resembles fine breadcrumbs.

Bring the mixture together to form a ball, and press it evenly over the base of the prepared brownie pan.

Transfer the pan to the oven and bake for 15 minutes until golden and firm.

Meanwhile, for the topping, beat the yogurt, sugar and lemon zest and juice together in a large bowl. Add the eggs, egg yolks and flour, and beat together until smooth.

Remove the base from the oven and immediately pour over the yogurt mixture in an even layer. Return the pan to the oven and bake for 30 minutes until the topping is set and golden.

Cool in the pan, and then cut into squares to serve.

GLUTEN-FREE LEMON & POPPY SEED DRIZZLE LOAF

Loaf cakes slice well and their smaller size and simplicity means they are the perfect option for those 'just because' days when a bake seems essential, but there's no particular celebration in the offing. That tangy lemon drizzle is always irresistible.

240 ml/1 cup whole/full-fat milk
1 tablespoon sunflower oil
2 eggs
260 g/1¾ cups plain/all-purpose gluten-free flour
3½ teaspoons baking powder
¼ teaspoon salt
⅜ teaspoon xanthan gum
250 g/1¼ cups caster/granulated sugar
grated zest of 2 lemons
70 g/5 tablespoons unsalted butter, softened, plus extra for greasing
2 tablespoons poppy seeds
crème fraîche, to serve

GLAZE
freshly squeezed juice of 2 lemons
100 g/½ cup caster/granulated sugar

900-g/2-lb. loaf pan, greased and lined

MAKES 1 LOAF CAKE

Preheat the oven to 180°C (350°F) Gas 4.

In a jug/pitcher, combine the milk, oil and eggs.

Place the flour, baking powder, salt, xanthan gum, sugar, lemon zest and softened butter in the bowl of a stand mixer (or use a large mixing bowl and a hand-held electric whisk). Slowly mix the dry ingredients and butter on low speed until the mixture resembles fine breadcrumbs.

Continue to mix on a slow speed and pour in the wet ingredients. Once combined, turn the speed to medium and mix for 3–5 minutes until the batter thickens. Add the poppy seeds and mix until they are evenly distributed.

Pour the batter into the loaf pan and level the top.

Bake in the preheated oven for 40–45 minutes until it is risen, golden and springs back when pressed lightly on the top, and a skewer inserted into the centre comes out clean. Put the pan onto a wire rack and allow to rest for 1–2 minutes while you mix together the glaze.

Stir the lemon juice and sugar together in a bowl. Leave the cake in the pan and prick the surface all over with a fork or skewer. Pour over the glaze – it's important to do this while the cake is still warm.

Leave the cake to cool completely in the pan on the wire rack, by which the time the glaze will have crystallized and set.

Remove the loaf from the pan. Slice and serve with a dollop of crème fraîche.

LEMON & YUZU MERINGUE TART

The classic tarte au citron is updated here with an unusual flavour. Yuzu is a Japanese citrus fruit, like a hybrid of lemon and lime with a hint of mandarin. The tart is topped with meringue, piped high and flambéed at the dinner table with a blowtorch!

a sheet of ready-rolled
    shortcrust pastry
25 g/1 oz. white chocolate

LEMON & YUZU CURD
2 tablespoons yuzu juice (available
    online or in good Japanese
    supermarkets)
grated zest and freshly squeezed
    juice of 2 lemons
3 egg yolks
100 g/½ cup raw cane sugar
2 tablespoons butter, chilled and
    diced

MERINGUE TOPPING
100 g/½ cup caster/superfine sugar
3 egg whites

20-cm/8-inch fluted tart pan,
    greased and lightly dusted
    with flour
baking beans
sugar thermometer
piping/pastry bag fitted with
    a plain nozzle/tip
kitchen blowtorch (optional)

SERVES 6–8

Preheat the oven to 180°C (350°F) Gas 4.

Unroll the pastry on a lightly floured surface and cut out a rough circle at about 25 cm/10 inches in diameter.

Transfer it to the prepared tart pan and gently coax the pastry neatly into the curves and angles of the pan. Press lightly into the sides and cut off any excess with a small, sharp knife.

Lay a sheet of greaseproof paper over the pan and fill it with baking beans. Put the pan on a baking sheet and bake in the preheated oven for 10–15 minutes.

Lower the oven temperature to 160°C (325°F) Gas 3. Remove the paper and beans from the tart pan and return the tart case to the oven for 5–10 minutes.

Allow to cool completely, then remove from the pan.

Meanwhile, melt the chocolate on low power in a microwave or in a heatproof bowl over a pan of simmering water (not letting the base of the bowl touch the water).

Brush the melted chocolate inside the cooled tart case.

For the lemon and yuzu curd, put the yuzu juice, juice of 1 lemon and all the lemon zest in a saucepan and bring to the boil over a low heat.

Put the egg yolks and sugar in a mixing bowl and whisk with a balloon whisk until it looks like the sugar has dissolved.

Very slowly pour the boiled citrus juice into the mixing bowl, whisking constantly. Pour the mixture back into the pan, set over a medium heat and stir. It will start to thicken and resemble thick, glossy curd.

Remove it from the heat and whisk in the butter, one piece at a time. Mix until all the butter has melted.

Pour the curd into the tart case and allow to cool completely.

For the meringue, put the sugar and 2 tablespoons water in a saucepan and bring to the boil. Simmer over low heat until the syrup reaches 121°C/250° on a sugar thermometer.

Meanwhile, put the egg whites and remaining lemon juice in a stand mixer and whisk until stiff peaks form

Once the syrup has reached the right temperature, slowly pour it in a steady stream into the meringue bowl with the beaters still running. Avoid letting the syrup touch the beaters. Keep whisking until you have used up all the syrup and the meringue is glossy, thick and has cooled substantially – this may take several minutes of whisking. The bowl itself must have cooled too.

Fill the piping bag with meringue and pipe the meringue onto the curd in the tart case.

To serve, blast the meringue with a kitchen blowtorch or place under a very hot grill/broiler.

BLACK COCONUT QUINOA
WITH GRIDDLED MANGO & MAKRUT LIME SYRUP

This is one of those super-versatile recipes that could be served at breakfast, brunch or even as a dessert. For dessert it's great with some ice cream and toasted coconut.

200 g/generous 1 cup black quinoa
300 ml/1¼ cups coconut cream
80 g/3 oz. palm sugar/jaggery
3 makrut lime leaves
1 lemongrass stalk, bashed
edible flowers, to decorate
    (optional)

MAKRUT LIME SYRUP
100 g/½ cup caster/granulated
    sugar
finely grated zest and freshly
    squeezed juice of 4 limes
20 makrut lime leaves, coarsely torn

GRIDDLED MANGO
2 firm mangoes, halved
2 tablespoons palm sugar/jaggery

SERVES 4

Rinse the quinoa under cold running water, place in a saucepan and cover generously with cold water. Bring to the boil over a medium–high heat and cook for about 10 minutes, or until tender. Drain well, and then set aside to cool slightly.

Meanwhile, for the makrut lime syrup, stir the sugar, lime juice and zest and 150 ml/⅔ cup water together in a saucepan over a medium heat to dissolve the sugar, then simmer until combined. Remove from the heat, add the makrut lime leaves and set aside to infuse for 1 hour, then strain into a jug/pitcher.

Heat a griddle/grill pan over a high heat. Sprinkle the mango halves with palm sugar and griddle/grill for a few minutes to char and caramelize the mango for flavour (not cook all the way through).

In another saucepan gently heat the coconut cream with the palm sugar, makrut lime leaves and lemongrass stalk, then add the quinoa and heat through. Remove and discard the lime leaves and lemongrass stalk.

Divide amongst serving bowls, top with griddled mango, drizzle with the syrup to taste (serving any extra syrup on the side) and decorate with edible flowers, if liked.

COCONUT & LIME RISOTTO
WITH BLACKBERRIES & BROWN SUGAR

Carnaroli risotto rice and coconut milk are great storecupboard staples to transform into a splendid dessert featuring inky blackberries and vibrant lime zest.

150 g/¾ cup carnaroli rice
3 x 400-ml/14-oz. cans full-fat
    coconut milk
50 g/¼ cup caster/superfine sugar
a pinch of salt
2 fresh bay leaves
2 tablespoons muscovado sugar
200 g/1½ cups blackberries
grated zest of 1 lime

SERVES 4

Preheat the oven to 190°C (375°F) Gas 5.

Put the rice into a deep roasting pan and stir in the milk, squashing any big lumps down with the tines of a fork (smaller lumps will amalgamate as the mixture cooks). Add the sugar, salt and bay leaves.

Bake for 20 minutes, then give it a stir and add a dash of water if it seems to need more liquid.

Bake for a further 15–20 minutes until the rice is soft and creamy.

Remove the pan from the oven and scatter over the muscovado sugar, swirling it gently with a fork to create a rippled effect.

Scatter with the blackberries and lime zest, and serve.

BLOOD ORANGE & CARAMEL BAKED CUSTARDS

When in season, blood oranges are utterly delicious, although a good orange flan can be made with any fresh orange juice that has a touch of lively acidity. This recipe is based on a traditional Spanish flan or baked custard.

600 ml/2½ cups freshly squeezed blood orange juice
200 g/1 cup caster/superfine sugar
grated zest of ½ orange
8 large/US extra-large egg yolks
2 medium/US large eggs

CARAMEL
150 g/¾ cup caster/superfine sugar

6 crème caramel moulds or other suitably sized ramekin dishes
an ovenproof baking dish, large enough to take the 6 moulds

MAKES 6

Preheat the oven to 180°C (350°F) Gas 4.

First make the caramel. Place the sugar and 150 ml/⅔ cup water in a saucepan. Start heating over a medium heat to dissolve the sugar completely. Increase the heat and bring to the boil without stirring. Cook rapidly until the syrup has taken a brick colour. Remove from the heat and pour carefully over the bottom and the sides of each mould. Place the moulds in a baking dish and set aside.

Place the orange juice, sugar and orange zest in another saucepan. Stir to dissolve the sugar in the water. Slowly bring to the boil, then reduce the heat to a very gentle simmer. Cook for a few minutes more, then remove from the heat and set aside.

Use a metal whisk to blend the egg yolks and whole eggs in a large bowl. Strain the sugary orange juice, then add to the eggs. Stir and strain into a jug/pitcher and pour into each mould.

Pour boiling water into the baking dish to come halfway up the sides of each mould. Cover the dish with aluminium foil and cook in the preheated oven for about 1 hour until the flans are set.

Remove the moulds from the water, leave to cool down, then place in the fridge for a couple of hours or even better overnight before serving.

FRAGRANT BLOOD ORANGE & ALMOND CAKE

This fragrant cake doesn't contain any flour, which helps give it an irresistible, dense but light texture. You can use ordinary oranges, but blood oranges have such a beautiful colour when they're in season, it's really worth seeking them out.

150 g/1¼ sticks butter, softened
300 g/1½ cups caster/superfine sugar
60 g/scant ¼ cup honey
5 eggs
200 g/1⅓ cups semolina or fine polenta/cornmeal
100 g/1 cup ground almonds
½ teaspoon baking powder
4 blood oranges
4 tablespoon marmalade

a 30 x 17 x 2.5cm/11¾ x 6¾ x 1 inch brownie pan, lightly greased and lined with baking parchment

MAKES 15

Preheat the oven to 170°C (325°F) Gas 3.

Whisk the butter and sugar in a bowl until light and fluffy. Whisk in the honey, then add the eggs, one at a time, whisking between each addition, until fully incorporated. If the mixture starts to look a little curdled, simply add some of the semolina and ground almonds.

Stir in the remaining semolina and ground almonds, together with the baking powder. Grate the zest from two of the oranges and add this into the mixture.

Spoon everything into the prepared brownie pan.

Top and tail the oranges, stand them on a cutting board and carefully slice away the peel, taking care to remove all of the pith. Thinly slice the oranges and arrange them lightly over the top of the cake mixture.

Bake for 35 minutes, or until a skewer inserted into the centre of the cake comes out clean, and the cake is golden and springy.

Push the marmalade through a fine sieve/strainer to remove any peel, and brush it liberally over the hot cake. Leave the cake to cool completely, before cutting into squares to serve.

SYRUPY CHEESE SPONGES
WITH CANDIED ORANGE & LEMON

These delectable cheese sponges can be served on their own as a sweet snack, as the finale to Mediterranean mezze selection or as a prominent part of the spread. Syrupy, with a hint of salt from the feta, the sponges are very moist and moreish and add an intriguing and satisfying touch to the meal.

125 g/1 scant cup plain/all-purpose or semolina flour
1 tablespoon icing/confectioners' sugar
1 scant teaspoon bicarbonate of soda/baking soda
50 g/3½ tablespoons butter
200 g/7 oz. feta, crumbled
1 egg

SYRUP
225 g/1 cup plus 1 tablespoon granulated sugar
freshly squeezed juice of 1 lemon, plus the rind finely shredded into thin threads
rind of 1 orange, finely shredded into thin threads

baking pan, lightly greased

SERVES 6

Preheat the oven to 180°C (360°F) Gas 4.

Start by making the syrup. Heat the sugar and 240 ml/1 cup water in a heavy-based pan, stirring all the time until the sugar has dissolved. Bring the water to the boil, stir in the lemon juice and both of the shredded rinds. Reduce the heat and simmer for 15–20 minutes.

Meanwhile, sift the flour, icing sugar, and bicarbonate of soda into a bowl and rub in the butter until it resembles fine breadcrumbs. Make a hollow in the middle and drop in the feta and the egg. Draw the flour over the top and, using your hands, knead the mixture into a sticky dough.

Rinse your hands, but keep them dampened. Mould the dough into small balls and place them at intervals in the greased baking pan – they need a little room to expand.

Bake in the preheated oven for 25 minutes.

Pour the hot syrup over the sponges, making sure they are all covered with the candied rind, and return them to the oven for 5–10 minutes.

Leave the sponges to cool in the baking pan and soak up the syrup.

Serve the sponges chilled or at room temperature.

CHOCOLATE MUD CAKE
WITH WHISKY & BLOOD ORANGE CREAM

This cake is dense, deep, moist, decadent, rich but not very sweet.
Serving it with a boozy whisky and blood orange cream makes it very grown up.

250 g/2¼ sticks unsalted butter,
    chopped
200 g/7 oz. dark/bittersweet
    chocolate, chopped
250 ml/1 cup full-fat/whole milk
80 ml/⅓ cup whisky or brandy
330 g/1½ cups plus 2 tablespoons
    caster/granulated sugar
1 teaspoon pure vanilla extract
1 teaspoon instant coffee
3 eggs
200 g/1½ cups plain/all-purpose
    flour, sifted
60 g/scant ½ cup self-raising/
    self-rising flour, sifted
2 tablespoons cocoa powder,
    sifted, plus extra for dusting
Crispy Blood Oranges, to serve
    (see page 171)

CHOCOLATE GANACHE ICING
150 g/5 oz. dark/bittersweet
    chocolate, chopped
1–2 teaspoons golden/light corn
    syrup, or to taste
125 ml/½ cup double/heavy cream

WHISKY & BLOOD ORANGE CREAM
200 ml/scant 1 cup double/heavy
    cream
4 teaspoons whisky or brandy
freshly squeezed juice of
    1 blood orange
2–3 tablespoons caster/superfine
    sugar, or to taste

*28 x 20-cm/11 x 8-inch baking pan,
    lightly greased*

SERVES 10

Preheat the oven to 150°C (300°F) Gas 2.

Place the butter, chocolate, milk, whisky, sugar, vanilla and coffee in a large pan over a medium heat and stir occasionally for 6 minutes until melted and smooth. Let cool slightly, then add the eggs and whisk to combine. Pour into a large bowl, add the flours and cocoa and whisk until smooth.

Pour into the prepared baking pan and bake in the preheated oven for 40 minutes, or until a skewer inserted in the centre comes out clean. Allow to cool completely in the pan, then remove.

To make the chocolate ganache icing, heat the chocolate, syrup and cream in a small pan over a low heat, stirring, until melted and smooth. Let cool completely.

For the blood orange cream, whisk the cream, whisky, blood orange juice and sugar until light and fluffy.

When the cake has cooled, spread the ganache icing over the top and allow to set. Serve with the blood orange cream and some crispy blood oranges.

FLOURLESS ALMOND & ORANGE CAKE

Oh for oranges and almonds... sigh. This cake, despite being flourless, remains deliciously moist and the puréed whole oranges give it a sharp vibrancy that is hard to beat. You can decorate it as here for special occasions, but it is also lovely as it is, if you don't have the time for the decoration.

4 oranges
400 g/4 cups ground almonds
1½ teaspoons baking powder
400 g/2 cups caster/superfine
   or granulated sugar
finely grated zest and freshly
   squeezed juice of ½ lemon
12 UK small/US medium eggs

GLAZE AND DECORATION
6 tablespoons apricot conserve
1 tablespoon brandy
250 ml/1 cup Greek yogurt
1 tablespoon caster/superfine sugar
grated zest of ½ orange
grated zest of ½ lemon
½–1 orange, peeled and segmented
1 tablespoon coarsely chopped
   shelled, unsalted pistachios
icing/confectioners' sugar, to dust
   (optional)

*a 22-cm/8½-inch diameter
   springform cake pan, lightly
   greased with butter*

SERVES 8

Bring a large pan of water to the boil, add the oranges whole and boil them for 2 hours, topping up the water as necessary to keep them fully submerged.

Once soft, gently lift the oranges out of the water and let cool for 10 minutes before putting in a blender. Pulse until they are a pulp and then pass this through a fine sieve/strainer set over a bowl, pushing it through with the back of a spoon. Set aside.

Preheat the oven to 200°C (400°F) Gas 6.

Combine the ground almonds, baking powder and sugar in a large mixing bowl. Stir in the strained orange pulp, add a small squeeze of lemon juice and mix to combine.

Whisk the eggs and pass through a coarse sieve/strainer directly into the bowl. Beat until incorporated.

Pour the mixture into the prepared cake pan. Bake in the preheated oven for 30 minutes, then remove and let cool in the pan.

To make the glaze, put the apricot conserve in a small bowl with the brandy, add 1 tablespoon cold water and stir to combine. Brush this glaze over the cooled cake to give it a little shine.

Put the yogurt and caster sugar in a bowl and stir to dissolve the sugar.

Decorate the cake by spooning the sweetened yogurt over the cake, arrange the orange segments on top and finish with the pistachios and a sprinkle of orange and lemon zest. Adding a dusting of icing/confectioners' sugar is optional.

MANGO & LIME JELLIES

Colourful, light and delicious, a classic combination after
a large meal. Serve with cream, if liked.

2 large ripe mangoes, pitted, peeled
    and roughly chopped
7 tablespoons caster/granulated
    sugar
20 g leaf gelatine/4 gelatin sheets
5 tablespoons Muscat dessert wine
3 tablespoons freshly squeezed
    lime juice
finely grated zest of 1 lime

TO SERVE
thin lime slices, dried in a low oven
200 ml/scant 1 cup single/light
    cream (optional)

SERVES 4

Put the mango flesh in a food
processor with the sugar and purée
until smooth.

Place the purée in a medium pan
and heat gently.

Soak the gelatine in plenty of cold
water for 5 minutes. Drain and
squeeze the gelatine and place
in the pan with the mango purée.
Stir until dissolved. Add 500 ml/
generous 2 cups water, the dessert
wine, lime juice and zest.

Mix thoroughly, pour into tall
glasses and chill for 6 hours.

Serve decorated with dried lime
slices and cream, if desired.

ZESTY LEMONADE & LEMON GRANITA

Who can resist a full glass of lemonade in the middle of the summer and what about a full glass of lemon granita after dinner? Unlike orange trees, lemon trees yield lemons all year round so these recipes can be enjoyed whatever the season.

3 large lemons, washed
300 g/1½ cups caster/superfine sugar
mint leaves, to garnish (optional)

MAKES 1.5 LITRES/6 CUPS

TO MAKE LEMONADE

Grate the zest of one of the lemons into a bowl. Cut all the lemons in half and squeeze the juice into the bowl. Add the squeezed lemon halves to the bowl, add 1.5 litres/ 6 cups water, stir and press the lemons as much as possible. Leave to macerate for 35 minutes.

Strain into a glass jar. Add about two-thirds of the sugar and then more to taste if needed. Stir well, then place in the fridge until ready to serve.

TO MAKE LEMON GRANITA

Follow the same method as for lemonade (see left) but instead of pouring the lemonade into a glass jar, pour into a light, freezerproof rectangular dish and place in the freezer for 30 minutes.

Remove from the freezer. By now some of the top should have converted into ice. Use the tines of a fork to break the ice by punching the surface and blending at the same time with the rest of the liquid. Return to the freezer for another 30 minutes and do the same again. Return it again to the freezer and repeat the freezing and blending until you have a truly fluffy granita.

Serve in pretty glasses such as the old traditional-style Champagne coupes. Add a little mint leaf to each glass before serving.

LIME & MINT GRANITA

This ice-cold granita couldn't be more refreshing.
Serve on a warm summer's day. Best enjoyed al fresco.

150 g/¾ cup granulated sugar
grated zest of 2 limes
100 ml/scant ½ cup freshly
squeezed lime juice
90 g/4½ cups fresh mint
lime slices, to serve

SERVES 8

Pour 600 ml/2½ cups cold water into a small saucepan, add the sugar and lime zest and bring the mixture to a simmer. Cook, stirring, until the sugar has dissolved.

Add half the mint (there's no need to chop or remove stalks) to the saucepan, then take it off the heat. Cover with a lid and allow to stand for 10 minutes, then remove the lid and let cool to room temperature.

Once cool, strain the mixture through a sieve/strainer into a large jug/pitcher, pressing firmly on the mint to extract the flavour. Stir the lime juice into the mint syrup, then pour into a light, freezerproof rectangular dish and place in the freezer for 1 hour.

Remove from the freezer. By now some of the top should have converted into ice. Use the tines of a fork to break the ice by punching the surface and blending at the same time with the rest of the liquid. Return to the freezer for another 30 minutes and do the same again. Return it again to the freezer and repeat the freezing and blending until you have a truly fluffy granita.

Serve in small glasses decorated with the remaining sprigs of mint and lime slices.

MANDARIN SORBET

Like the lemon sorbet, mandarin sorbet is a great palate cleanser and so is perfect for enjoying between courses at a celebration dinner. Amongst all the delicious mandarin varieties, clementines are the best choice when in season.

340 ml/1½ cups spring water
freshly squeezed juice of ½ lemon
180 g/¾ cup plus 2 tablespoons
  caster/superfine sugar
400 ml/1⅔ cups freshly squeezed
  mandarin juice

SERVES 4

In a saucepan set over a medium heat, gently heat 160 ml/⅔ cup of the spring water until it reaches boiling point. Remove from the heat, add the lemon juice and stir in all but 2 tablespoons of the sugar until it dissolves. Let the syrup cool for 30 minutes.

Put the mandarin juice and the remaining water and sugar in a jug/pitcher and whisk them together. Add the cooled syrup and whisk briefly again until thoroughly mixed.

Pour the mixture into an ice cream maker and churn freeze according to the manufacturer's instructions.

The sorbet is best served immediately, or can be kept in the freezer for 3–4 days.

CANDIED CITRUS SEMIFREDDO

The really great thing about making a semifreddo is that you don't need an ice cream maker. It freezes wonderfully in a container and you can serve it either in scoops or turned out onto a serving plate and sliced.

3 eggs
2 egg yolks
100 g/½ cup caster/superfine sugar
500 ml/2 cups double/heavy cream
3 tablespoons candied citrus,
    finely chopped

SERVES 6–8

Combine the eggs, yolks, and sugar in a heatproof bowl and place over a pot of simmering water. Whisk with an electric hand whisk on a high speed for about 5 minutes, until it turns into pale yellow ribbons and has thickened.

Turn off the heat and place the bowl over a bowl filled with iced water to cool.

Meanwhile, pour the cream into a large bowl and beat until thick, and soft peaks form.

Fold the cooled egg mixture through the cream until thoroughly incorporated. Fold in the candied fruit and pour into a clean bowl. Cover with clingfilm/plastic wrap and freeze until firm.

LEMON SORBET
WITH CANDIED CITRUS

Ubiquitous across the Mediterranean where the lemons are sweet and delicious, lemon sorbet is such a crowd-pleaser. Serving it in a lemon makes it more elegant.

330 g/1⅓ cups golden caster/granulated sugar
250 ml/1 cup freshly squeezed lemon juice (i.e. juice of 10 lemons)
100 ml/7 tablespoons limoncello
6–8 lemon halves, hollowed out and frozen

SERVES 6–8

Stir the sugar and 375 ml/1½ cups of water in a medium saucepan over medium–high heat until the sugar dissolves. Bring to the boil and cook for 2 minutes. Cool completely – you can do this a day in advance.

Add the lemon juice, limoncello and 250 ml/1 cup water to the sugar syrup. Stir to combine.

Freeze and churn in an ice-cream machine. Alternatively, freeze in a metal container and, after 2 hours, fork over to break up the ice crystals. Repeat every 2 hours until you have a fine sorbet texture.

Serve in frozen lemon halves.

LIMONATA
SICILIAN LEMON SYRUP

Making the most of their legendary lemons, this refreshing, fragrant drink is enjoyed all over Sicily with various treats. If you prefer a sweeter version, add another 50 g/3 tablespoons of sugar.

250 g/1¼ cups golden caster/granulated sugar
10 basil leaves
grated zest of 5 lemons
freshly squeezed juice of 15 lemons

MAKES 350 ML/1½ CUPS

In a medium saucepan, mix the sugar and 200 ml/¾ cup water together and set over a gentle heat to dissolve the sugar.

When the sugar has dissolved, add the basil leaves and leave to infuse until the sugar syrup is cold, then remove the basil.

Add the lemon zest and juice, and mix well.

To serve, mix with sparkling/soda water for a perfect Sicilian lemonade or even used in cocktails.

Store in the fridge for 4 weeks, but it really won't last that long!

4

DRINKS & PRESERVES

SALTY LIME SODA

The inspiration for this thirst-quenching drink comes from India, where it is enjoyed as a refresher in the sweltering heat. It is simple to make and makes a tasty change to usual lime sodas – give it a try!

4 teaspoons good-quality sea salt
grated zest and freshly squeezed
   juice of 4 limes
400-ml/14-oz. bottle of soda water
ice and lime slices, to serve

SERVES 2

Mix together the salt, lime zest and juice and soda water in a jug/pitcher. Pour into long tall glasses, and serve with ice and lime.

LEMON & GINGER BARLEY WATER

This is oh so good for you. Barley and ginger are full of therapeutic properties, and of course lemons are full of vitamin C.

125 g/⅔ cup pot barley
grated zest and freshly squeezed
   juice of 4 lemons
100 g/½ cup brown sugar
5-cm/2-inch piece of fresh ginger,
   peeled and roughly grated
1.2 litres/5 cups boiling water
ice and lime slices, to serve

SERVES 4

Wash the barley and place in a large heatproof jug/pitcher with the lemon zest, sugar and ginger. Pour the boiling water over the mixture and allow to cool for several hours.

When the mixture is cold, add the juice of the lemons. Strain and then serve in a glass with ice and lime.

LEMON & MINT SODA

This fizzy lemonade will forever change the way you think about soda! It's a hundred times tastier than all the commercial sodas out there and it's so refreshing you'll be reaching for it all summer long.

4 tablespoons water kefir
100 g/½ cup raw cane sugar
  or other sweetener
1–2 lemons, peeled
a handful of mint leaves

1.5-litre/quart preserving jar
  with tight-fitting lid
1.5-litre/quart glass bottle
  or another 1.5-litre/quart
  preserving jar

MAKES 1.5 LITRES/6 CUPS

Put the water kefir grains in the jar, add the sweetener and 1 litre/4 cups water and stir well.

Cut each lemon into 8 slices and add to the jar together with the mint leaves. Seal with the jar lid.

Keep the jar away from direct sunlight and leave to ferment for 2 days, stirring a couple of times in those 48 hours. Be careful when opening the jar because a lot of carbon dioxide will be produced by the fermentation!

Strain the liquid into a clean bottle or jar, squeeze out all the juice from lemon slices and add it, then discard the used lemon and mint leaves. Rinse the kefir grains and re-use.

If you're not going to drink this soda right away, refrigerate and make sure it is well sealed to keep it fizzy.

SUNDAY MOJITO

This is the fruitiest and most refreshing variation on a minty mojito recipe you'll ever need. (Pictured on page 161.)

1 lime, cut into eighths
4 lychees (from a can)
a generous handful of mint leaves
90 ml/6 tablespoons Malibu
30 ml/2 tablespoons lychee liqueur
160 ml/⅔ cup pineapple juice
pineapple leaves, to garnish

SERVES 2

Place the lime wedges into a cocktail shaker. Using a muddler, gently crush the lime with the lychees and mint leaves.

Add the Malibu, lychee liqueur and plenty of ice. Shake vigorously.

Strain into highball glasses and top up with the pineapple juice.

LIMONCELLO APERITIF

This is a wonderful ice-breaking cocktail, perfect served as an aperitif at the start of a dinner party.

2 tablespoons limoncello
Prosecco, to top
ice, lemon slice and a sprig
of mint, to serve

SERVES 1

Pour the Limoncello into a large wine glass and top up with Prosecco. Add the ice, lemon slice and mint. Serve at once.

PALOMA

The combination of lime and grapefruit is a match made in citrus heaven.

100 ml/7 tablespoons tequila
150 ml/⅔ cup pink grapefruit juice
4 teaspoons freshly squeezed lime
juice
2 teaspoons vanilla sugar
ice, lime and grapefruit wedges,
to serve

SERVES 2

Add the tequila, fruit juices and sugar to a shaker with ice cubes and shake.

Strain into highball glasses filled with ice cubes. Garnish with lime and grapefruit wedges.

THE CAPRI

Campari brings such a refreshing herbal tone to any cocktail and it doesn't disappoint here. You can use tangerines, oranges, kumquats, or mandarins in this cocktail – it's a fun way to drink round the year with whatever is in season.

2 tangerines
60 ml/¼ cup Hendrick's gin
60 ml/¼ cup Campari
1 tablespoon freshly squeezed
    lemon juice
450 g/2 cups ice cubes
sprigs of lavender, to garnish
    (optional)

SIMPLE SYRUP
200 g/1 cup white sugar

SERVES 4

To make the simple syrup, place the sugar and 250 ml/1 cup water in a saucepan and bring to the boil over medium–high heat. Reduce the heat and simmer until the sugar has dissolved.

Remove from the heat and cool. Store in a jar with a lid in the fridge.

Place the unpeeled tangerines, gin, Campari, lemon juice, and 60 ml/¼ cup of the simple syrup in a blender along with the ice cubes. Process until smooth.

Pour into chilled glasses and garnish with lavender sprigs, if using.

PISCO SOUR

The Pisco Sour originates in Lima and it could be considered Peru's national drink. Pisco – a spirit distilled from grapes – has a bright, lively flavour with grape aromatics. Mixed with lime, it makes a really nice cocktail.

ice
120 ml/½ cup Pisco
60 ml/¼ cup freshly squeezed
    lime juice (Key limes if possible)
2 egg whites
3 tablespoons simple syrup
    (see above)
a dash of angostura bitters
lime wheels, to serve

MAKES 2

Fill a cocktail shaker with ice and pour in the Pisco, lime juice, egg whites and simple syrup. Shake vigorously and strain into two glasses.

Top with a dash of angostura bitters and garnish with lime wheels.

BOBBIE'S FIZZ

This is such a wonderful way to finish a meal. Tangy kumquat sorbet floating in icy Prosecco – it tastes even better than it looks. Serve in vintage coupe glasses for evening elegance and in small tumblers for a casual barbecue.

24 kumquats, tops trimmed
400 g/2 cups caster/superfine sugar
1 tablespoon freshly squeezed
    lemon juice
a pinch of sea salt
Prosecco, chilled, to top

SERVES 6

Place the kumquats in a medium pan and cover with water. Bring to the boil over a high heat, then drain. Repeat the procedure twice more – this will reduce the bitterness of the peel. Set aside.

Bring the sugar and 500 ml/2 cups water to the boil in a pan over medium–high heat, stirring to dissolve the sugar. Reduce the heat to a simmer and cook for 5 minutes until the sugar has completely dissolved. Set aside to cool slightly.

Pour the sugar syrup into a blender with the kumquats and add the lemon juice and salt. Purée until smooth. Cover and set aside to cool, then refrigerate for 2 hours.

Freeze the mixture in an ice cream maker according to the manufacturer's instructions. Store in an airtight container in the freezer until ready to use.

To serve, add a scoop of sorbet to each glass and pour the Prosecco over the top.

MEYER LIMONCELLO CHAMPAGNE COCKTAIL

Wonderful citrus Meyer Limoncello meets bubbles – a fun, refreshing drink to kick off cocktail hour. This is great served at parties as it is simple and fuss-free.

Meyer Limoncello (see right),
    chilled
Champagne, chilled, to top

SERVES 6

Pour a splash of Meyer Limoncello in the bottom of six chilled Champagne glasses and top with the Champagne. Serve at once.

MEYER LIMONCELLO

12 Meyer lemons
750 ml/3¼ cups vodka

SYRUP
200 g/1 cup caster/superfine sugar

a large sterilized glass jar
sterilized bottles with airtight lids

SERVES 6

Peel the lemon skin with a sharp vegetable peeler, avoiding the pith. Squeeze the juice from the lemons into a large sterilized glass jar and add the peel. Pour in the vodka

and stir. Cover and set aside at room temperature for 2 weeks. To make the syrup, bring the sugar and 350 ml/1½ cups water to the boil in a saucepan over medium–high heat. Reduce the heat and simmer for 10 minutes, stirring occasionally until the sugar has dissolved. Allow to cool.

Add the syrup to the Limoncello mixture. Set aside for 30 minutes.

Strain though a muslin/cheesecloth into a jug/pitcher, then decant into sterilized bottles and store in the refrigerator for up to 12 months.

LEMONS PRESERVED IN SALT

Salt is a natural preserver and has been since ancient times. When it comes to food, though, salt is a saviour – a miraculous preserver of meat, fish, vegetables and fruit – and perhaps the best example of all are lemons preserved in salt. Most commonly associated with North Africa, preserved lemons are used throughout the Levant. The flavour is sublime and, generally, it is only the rind, finely chopped or thinly sliced, that is used to enhance salads, vegetable dishes and some roasted and grilled dishes. Preserved lemons are readily available in Middle Eastern stores but they are also very easy and satisfying to make at home.

8 unwaxed lemons
8 tablespoons sea salt
freshly squeezed juice of
**   3–4 lemons**

a large sterilized jar

Wash and dry the lemons and slice the ends off each one. Stand each lemon on one end and make two vertical cuts three-quarters of the way through them, as if cutting them into quarters but keeping the base intact. Use a spoon to stuff a tablespoon of salt into each lemon and pack them into a large sterilized jar. Store the lemons in a cool place for 3–4 days to soften the skins.

Press the lemons down into the jar, so they are even more tightly packed. Pour the freshly squeezed lemon juice over the salted lemons, until they are completely covered. Seal the jar and store it in a cool place for at least a month.

Rinse the salt off the preserved lemons before using as described in the recipes – just the rind, finely chopped or sliced, is used and the flesh is discarded.

LIME MARMALADE

As easy to make as to eat.

6 small limes
3 lemons
2 kg/10 cups granulated sugar

3 sterilized jars

MAKES 3 X 450-G/1-LB. JARS

Scrub the limes and lemons, cut into quarters and remove the seeds. Fill a large pan with 3 litres/12 cups of water and soak the fruit for 24 hours.

Remove the fruit from the pan and cut into small shreds. Return to the water in which it has been soaking, bring to the boil and boil for 1 hour.

Next add all the sugar to the pan. Boil again until the juice forms a jelly when tested.

To test if the marmalade is ready, place 2 teaspoons of the mixture on a cold saucer. Press the surface of the marmalade with your thumb and if it wrinkles, it is done. Let cool for 10 minutes.

Transfer the marmalade into sterilized jars and seal.

Store in a dark, cool place. For the best taste, allow the marmalade to set for 1 month.

LEMON BANANA CURD

This sweet, thick spread is wonderful on bread, ice cream or pancakes.

4 large bananas
125 g/1⅛ sticks butter
250 g/1¼ cups caster/superfine
   sugar
grated zest and freshly squeezed
   juice of 2 lemons
a pinch of ground ginger, or
   1 teaspoon chopped fresh ginger
4 eggs

2 sterilized jars

MAKES 2 X 450-G/1-LB. JARS

Peel the bananas, place in a bowl and mash with a fork.

Melt the butter in a saucepan, then add the sugar, bananas, lemon zest and juice and ginger. Cook gently over very low heat for 10 minutes.

Beat the eggs in a bowl, then gradually beat in 3 tablespoons of the banana mixture. Pour the egg mixture into the pan and continue stirring. Cook gently, stirring constantly, for 10 minutes, or until mixture coats the back of a wooden spoon. Do not boil.

Pour into sterilized jars and seal. Store in fridge and eat within 10 days.

CANDIED PEEL

There are literally hundreds and hundreds of recipes and variations for candied peel, but this recipe works well and tastes wonderful.

1 orange
1 lemon
1 grapefruit
**350 g/1¾ cups caster/
  granulated sugar**
**1 vanilla pod/bean,
  split lengthways**
1 star anise
1 cinnamon stick

MAKES 200 G/1½ CUPS

Using a sharp knife, cut the orange into 4 wedges and remove the flesh. Cut each piece of peel into 3–4 chunky strips. Repeat with the lemon and grapefruit.

Place the peels into a saucepan, cover with cold water and bring to the boil. Simmer for 10 minutes and then drain. Repeat this process twice more (this process removes the bitterness), then drain the peels and set aside while you prepare the sugar syrup.

Tip the sugar into a pan and add 350 ml/1½ cups water. Add the vanilla, star anise and cinnamon. Set over a medium heat to dissolve the sugar, stirring occasionally.

Add the peels to the pan and boil steadily for 40 minutes, stirring occasionally, until the peels become soft and translucent, and almost all of the syrup has been absorbed. Keep a close eye on the pan as it can burn.

Using tongs, remove the peels from the pan, one at a time, and lay on a sheet of parchment paper in a single layer. Cover and leave to dry overnight. They should no longer be sticky.

Store in a box or airtight container for up to 1 month.

Chop and add to cakes, biscuits, cookies and desserts, as required.

CRISPY BLOOD ORANGES

These crispy orange slices can be used as decoration on cakes and desserts and will infuse your kitchen with delightful citrussy aromas.

1–2 blood oranges
**1 tablespoon caster/
  superfine sugar**

Preheat the oven to 70·C (160°F) or the lowest gas setting.

Thinly slice the oranges (with the peel on), place on the baking sheet and sprinkle with sugar.

Place in the oven, keep the oven door slightly ajar and dehydrate them in the oven until crispy and dry – this usually takes a few hours.

INDEX

CREDITS

RECIPE CREDITS

VALERIE AIKMAN-SMITH
Bobbie's Fizz
Cajun Crispy Pork Belly
   with Kumquat Dipping
   Sauce
Candied Citrus Semifreddo
Meyer Limoncello
   Champagne Cocktail
Peppered Pan-fried Olives
Pisco Sour
The Capri

GHILLIE BASAN
Fish Stew with Tamarind,
   Hilbeh & Dried Limes
Lemons Preserved in Salt
Meatballs in an Egg
   & Lemon Sauce
Syrupy Cheese Sponges
   with Candied Orange
   & Lemon

ADRIANO DI PETRILLO
Mandarin Sorbet

URSULA FERRIGNO
Cabbage Leaves Stuffed
   with Gochujang & Lime
   Pork
Candied Peel
Citrus-marinated Ceviche
Crab, Chilli & Lemon
   Linguine
Deep-fried Baby Artichokes
   with Lemon, Mint &
   Anchovy Dressing
Key Lime Pie
Lemon Banana Curd
Lemon & Ginger Barley
   Water
Lemon, Cardamom
   & Raspberry Torte
Lemon, Fennel & Rocket
   Salad with Radicchio
Lemon Sorbet with
   Candied Citrus
Lime Marmalade

Lime & Mint Granita
Limonata Sicilian Lemon
Limoncello Aperitif
Lobster Tails with Lime
   Butter
Mango & Lime Jellies
Mussels with Samphire
Paloma
Peking Suck Salad
Pork Dumplings in Lime
   Leaf Broth
Pork Escalopes with
   Lemon Sauce
Salmon Escabeche
   with Celery & Citrus
Salty Lime Soda
Seabass with Roasted
   Red Pepper butter, Basil
   & Black Olives
Sunday Mojito
Thai-style King Prawns
Tuna Carpaccio with
   Lemon Parsley Sauce
Vietnamese Noodle Soup

AMY RUTH FINEGOLD
Avocado, Rocket &
   Grapefruit Salad with
   Sunflower Seeds

LIZ FRANKLIN
Caramelized Fennel
   & Heritage Carrots
Fragrant Blood Orange
   & Almond Cake
Lemon Yogurt Squares
Lime, Vegetable &
   Coconut Curry
Salt-baked Heritage
   Beetroot & Mango
   Lettuce Cups
Spring Vegetable Barigoule
   with Zingy Gremolata
Sweet Bay-scented
   Coconut & Lime with
   Blackberries & Brown
   Sugar

FELIPE FUENTES CRUZ
Chayote & Grapefruit Salad

DUNJA GULIN
Lemon & Mint Soda
Citrus Fruits with Lavender
Honey
Powerhouse Salad
Spicy & Sweet Salad with
Kumquats & Brazil Nuts

VICTORIA HALL
Gluten-free Lemon &
Poppy Seed Drizzle Loaf

CAROL HILKER
Lemon, Basil & Pepper
Wings

KATHY KORDALIS
Black Bean Rice with
Slow-Cooked Pork
Black Coconut Quinoa
with Griddled Mango
& Makrut Lime Syrup
Chocolate Mud Cake with
Whisky & Blood Orange
Cream
Coconut & Semolina
Cake with Citrus Syrup
Freekah & Herb Salad
with Preserved Lemon
& Black Olives
Stuffed Vine Leaves
Tamarind Rice Salad with
Crab & Green Chillies
Toasted Mixed Grains with
Lemon Labne
Wheatberries, Chorizo,
Orange, Olive &
Radicchio Salad

JENNY LINFORD
Sun-Blush Tomato,
Orange & Burrata Salad
Thai Tomato Salad

THEO A. MICHAELS
Avgolemono
Citrus Salad with
Rosewater Caramel
Cypriot Ful Medames with
Preserved Lemon Salsa
Home-cured Anchovies
Home-cured Duck
'Prosciutto'
Flourless Almond &
Orange Cake
Lemon Lamb en Papilotte
Oven-roasted Hake on
Citrusy Greens
Seville Lamb Riblets

LOUISE PICKFORD
Mexican Chicken & Lime
Soup
Pea & Ham Soup with
Lemon & Thyme Oil
Whole Pot Roast Chicken
with Lemon, Olives &
Sweet Spices

JAMES PORTER
Hawaiian Salmon Scraps
with Guava Ponzu
Poisson Cru
Sea Bass Crudo

SARAH RANDALL
Rosewater, Pistachio
& Grapefruit Cake

ANNIE RIGG
Clementine & Pistachio
Cakes

SHELAGH RYAN
Grilled Squid Salad with
Herb-Lime Dressing
Quinoa & Red Rice Salad

LAURA SANTINI
Artichoke, Lemon &
Parmesan Penne
Lemon, Mint & Caper
Spaghetti
Lemon Spaghetti
Smoked Mackerel & Pink
Peppercorn Pasta Salad

MARÍA JOSÉ SEVILLA
Blood Orange & Caramel
Baked Custards
Mussels with Lemon Zest
Orange Cream Roulade
Orange, Honey & Olive Oil
Salad
Orange-marinated Green
Olives
Ventresca of Red Tuna
with Orange Sauce
Zesty Lemonade & Lemon
Granita

WILL TORRENT
Lemon & Yuzu Meringue
Tart

JENNY TSCHIESCHE
Orange-Baked Rhubarb

**LAURA WASHBURN
HUTTON**
Grapefruit & Prawn salad

PHOTOGRAPHY
CREDITS

JAN BALDWIN
Page 139.

PETER CASSIDY
Page 3.

JONATHAN GREGSON
Page 131.

MOWIE KAY
Pages 1, 15, 16, 19, 20, 23,
41, 42, 45, 49, 65, 66, 75,
80, 83, 86, 103, 117, 123,
124, 132, 140, 141 and
143.

ERIN KUNKEL
Pages 2, 13, 69, 151, 162,
163 and 165.

ADRIAN LAWRENCE
Page 128.

DAVID MUNNS
Pages 27, 153 and 170.

STEVE PAINTER
Pages 12, 84, 99, 100, 107,
127, 136, 150 and 166.

NASSIMA ROTHACKER
Pages 6, 11, 46, 89, 91, 92,
119, 135, 146 and 147.

CHRISTOPHER SCHOLEY
Pages 95 and 104.

TOBY SCOTT
Pages 76 and 158.

IAN WALLACE
Pages 35, 36, 37, 38 and
79.

KATE WHITTAKER
Pages 55, 57, 59, 61, 77,
111, 112 and 115.

CLARE WINFIELD
Pages 5, 7, 24, 25, 26, 28,
33, 34, 44, 48, 50, 53, 54,
70, 72, 87, 88, 96, 106,
117, 120, 121, 125, 137,
144, 145, 148, 149, 156,
157, 160, 161, 168 and
169.